THE
PSYCHOLOGY
OF
THE CHILD

THE
PSYCHOLOGY
OF
THE CHILD

Jean Piaget

AND

Bärbel Inhelder

Translated from the French by HELEN WEAVER

ROUTLEDGE & KEGAN PAUL

London

Originally published in French as
La Psychologie de l'enfant
by Presses Universitaires de France, Paris. 1966
© *1966 by Presses Universitaires de France*
First published 1969 in the United States of America
by Basic Books, Inc.
First published in Great Britain 1969
by Routledge & Kegan Paul Ltd
Broadway House, 68–74 Carter Lane
London, EC4V 5EL
Reprinted 1971
Printed in Great Britain by
Lowe & Brydone (Printers) Ltd.
© *1969 by Basic Books, Inc.*
ISBN 0 7100 6751 8

PREFACE

IN THIS VOLUME we have tried to present, as briefly and as clearly as possible, a synthesis, or summing up, of our work in child psychology. A book such as this seemed to us particularly desirable since our published studies have been spread out over a number of volumes, some of them quite lengthy and some of them fairly difficult to read. This little book, of course, is not meant to be a substitute for reading the other volumes. But it represents, we believe, a useful introduction to the questions we have studied and will enable the reader to gain an adequate understanding of what we have learned in our investigations.

March 1969   Jean Piaget

                                          Bärbel Inhelder

INTRODUCTION

The Psychology of the Child deals with mental growth or, what amounts to the same thing, the development of behavior patterns (including consciousness) up to adolescence, the transitional phase marking the entrance of the individual into adult society. Mental growth is inseparable from physical growth: the maturation of the nervous and endocrine systems, in particular, continues until the age of sixteen. This implies that in order to understand mental growth it is not enough to start with birth; there is an embryology of reflexes (E. Minkowski) dealing with the movements and responses of the fetus, and the preperceptive behavior of the fetus, for instance, is relevant to the study of the perception of tactilo-kinesthetic causality.[1] From a theoretical point of view, it also implies that child psychology must be regarded as the study of one aspect of embryogenesis, the embryogenesis of organic as well as mental growth, up to the beginning of the state of relative equilibrium which is the adult level.

Organically as well as mentally, however, environmental influences assume increasing importance after birth. Child

[1] See A. Michotte, *The Perception of Causality* (New York: Basic Books, 1963).

psychology, in its search for factors of development, cannot be limited to a study of biological maturation. Other, equally important factors are to be considered—exercise or acquired experience as well as social life in general.

Child psychology studies the mental development of the child for its sake. In this respect it must be distinguished from "genetic psychology," although it constitutes the essential tool of this discipline. To dispel any ambiguity about terminology, let us note first that the word "genetic," as used in the expression "genetic psychology," was introduced by psychologists in the second half of the nineteenth century to refer to the developmental aspects of psychology. Later, biologists began to use the term "genetics" in a more restricted sense. In the current language of biologists, "genetics" refers only to the mechanisms of heredity and does not include the study of embryogenetic or developmental processes. The term "genetic psychology," however, continues to refer to individual development (ontogenesis).

As a result, one might be tempted to consider the expressions "child psychology" and "genetic psychology" to be synonymous, but there is an important distinction between them: Whereas child psychology deals with the child for his own sake and does not consider his eventual development into an adult, we tend today to use the term "genetic psychology" to refer to the study of the developmental processes that underlie the mental functions studied in general psychology (intelligence, perceptions, etc.). Genetic psychology tries to explain mental functions by their mode of formation; that is, by their development in the child.

For example, the study of logical thinking, its operations

and structures, in the completed state found in the adult led some authors (German *Denkpsychologie*) to believe that thinking was a "mirror of logic." Psychologists eventually began to wonder whether logic was innate or resulted from a gradual development. To solve problems of this kind they turn their study to the child and in so doing promote "child psychology" to the rank of "genetic psychology": "genetic psychology" becomes an essential tool of explicative analysis to solve the problems of general psychology.

The genetic method has become important in all branches of psychology (consider, for example, the major role attributed to childhood by psychoanalysis) and thus gives child psychology a key position in many diverse fields of psychology. In this work, therefore, we will speak primarily from the point of view of genetic psychology. The child is of considerable interest in himself, but interest in psychological investigations of the child is increased when we realize that the child explains the man as well as and often better than the man explains the child. While the adult educates the child by means of multiple social transmissions, every adult, even if he is a creative genius, nevertheless began as a child, in prehistoric times as well as today.

A*

CONTENTS

THE
PSYCHOLOGY
OF
THE CHILD

1

THE SENSORI-MOTOR LEVEL

IF THE CHILD partly explains the adult, it can also be said that each period of his development partly explains the periods that follow. This is particularly clear in the case of the period where language is still absent. We call it the "sensori-motor" period because the infant lacks the symbolic function; that is, he does not have representations by which he can evoke persons or objects in their absence. In spite of this lack, mental development during the first eighteen months[1] of life is particularly important, for it is during this time that the child constructs all the cognitive substructures that will serve as a point of departure for his later perceptive and intellectual development, as well as a certain number of elementary affective reactions that will partly determine his subsequent affectivity.

[1] Ages indicated in this book are always average and approximate.

I. *Sensori-motor Intelligence*

Whatever criteria for intelligence one adopts—purposeful groping (E. Claparède), sudden comprehension or insight (W. Köhler or K. Bühler), coordination of means and ends, etc.—everyone agrees in recognizing the existence of an intelligence before language. Essentially practical— that is, aimed at getting results rather than at stating truths —this intelligence nevertheless succeeds in eventually solving numerous problems of action (such as reaching distant or hidden objects) by constructing a complex system of action-schemes[2] and organizing reality in terms of spatio-temporal and causal structures. In the absence of language or symbolic function, however, these constructions are made with the sole support of perceptions and movements and thus by means of a sensori-motor coordination of actions, without the intervention of representation or thought.

1. *Stimulus-Response and Assimilation*

There certainly is such a thing as a sensori-motor intelligence, but it is very difficult to specify the exact moment when it appears. Actually, the question makes no sense, for the answer always depends upon an arbitrary choice of criterion. What one actually finds is a remarkably smooth succession of stages, each marking a new advance, until the moment when the acquired behavior presents charac-

---

[2] A scheme is the structure or organization of actions as they are transferred or generalized by repetition in similar or analogous circumstances.

teristics that one or another psychologist recognizes as those of "intelligence." (All writers are in agreement in attributing this quality to at least the last of these stages, from twelve to eighteen months.) There is a continuous progression from spontaneous movements and reflexes to acquired habits and from the latter to intelligence. The real problem is not to locate the first appearance of intelligence but rather to understand the mechanism of this progression.

For many psychologists this mechanism is one of association, a cumulative process by which conditionings are added to reflexes and many other acquisitions to the conditionings themselves. According to this view, every acquisition, from the simplest to the most complex, is regarded as a response to external stimuli, a response whose associative character expresses a complete control of development by external connections. One of us,[3] on the other hand, has argued that this mechanism consists in *assimilation* (comparable to biological assimilation in the broad sense): meaning that reality data are treated or modified in such a way as to become incorporated into the structure of the subject. In other words, every newly established connection is integrated into an existing schematism. According to this view, the organizing activity of the subject must be considered just as important as the connections inherent in the external stimuli, for the subject becomes aware of these connections only to the degree that he can assimilate them by means of his existing structures. In other words, associationism conceives the relationship between stimulus and response in a unilateral manner: $S \rightarrow R$; whereas

[3] Jean Piaget, *The Origins of Intelligence in Children* (New York: International Universities Press, 1951; London: Routledge and Kegan Paul, 1953).

the point of view of assimilation presupposes a reciprocity
$S \rightleftarrows R$; that is to say, the input, the stimulus, is filtered
through a structure that consists of the action-schemes (or,
at a higher level, the operations of thought), which in turn
are modified and enriched when the subject's behavioral
repertoire is accommodated to the demands of reality. The
filtering or modification of the input is called *assimilation*;
the modification of internal schemes to fit reality is called
accommodation.

2. *Stage 1*

The point of departure of development should not be
sought in the reflexes conceived as simple isolated responses, but in the spontaneous and total activities of the
organism (studied by E. von Holst and others). There are
relatively fixed and predictable reflexes embedded in this
total activity, but they can be viewed as a differentiation of
this global activity, as we shall see. Some of these reflexes
are developed by exercise instead of remaining unchanged
or atrophying and are the points of departure for the development of schemes of assimilation.

On the one hand, it has been shown by the study of
animal behavior as well as by the study of the electrical
activity of the nervous system that the organism is never
passive, but presents spontaneous and global activities
whose form is rhythmic. On the other hand, embryological
analysis of the reflexes (G. E. Coghill and others) has en-
abled us to establish the fact that reflexes are formed by
differentiation upon a groundwork of more global activities. In the case of the locomotive reflexes of the batra-
chians, for example, it is an overall rhythm which culminates in a succession of differentiated and coordinated

reflexes, and not the reflexes which lead to that rhythm.

As far as the reflexes of the newborn child are concerned, those among them that are of particular importance for the future (the sucking reflex and the palmar reflex, which will be integrated into later intentional grasping) give rise to what has been called a "reflex exercise"; that is, a consolidation by means of functional exercise. This explains why after a few days the newborn child nurses with more assurance and finds the nipple more easily when it has slipped out of his mouth than at the time of his first attempts.[4] The reproductive or functional assimilation that accounts for this exercise also gives rise to a generalizing assimilation (sucking on nothing between meals or sucking new objects) and a recognitive assimilation (distinguishing the nipple from other objects).

We cannot label these modifications of sucking acquisitions in a strict sense, since the assimilating exercise does not yet go beyond the preestablished boundaries of the hereditary apparatus. Nevertheless, the assimilation fulfills a fundamental role in developing this activity. This makes it impossible to regard the reflex as a pure automatism and also accounts for later extensions of the reflex scheme and for the formation of the first habits. In the case of sucking we observe, sometimes as early as the second month, the commonplace but nonetheless instructive phenomenon of a baby sucking his thumb. Fortuitous or accidental thumbsucking may occur as early as the first day. The more advanced sucking is systematic and dependent upon a coordination of the movements of arm, hand, and

[4] Similar reflex exercises are observed in animals too, as in the groping that characterizes the first efforts at copulation in Lymnaeae.

mouth. Associationists see here only an effect of repetition (but what is the source of this repetition, since it is not imposed by external connections?), and psychoanalysts already see a symbolic behavior by representative identification of the thumb and the breast (but what is the source of this symbolic or evocative power, well before the formation of the first mental images?). We suggest that this acquisition be interpreted as a simple extension of the sensorimotor assimilation at work as early as the reflex. It is quite clear that this is a genuine case of acquisition in a broad sense, since there exists no reflex or instinct for sucking one's thumb (indeed, the appearance of this activity and its frequency are subject to variation). But this acquisition is not a random affair: it is introduced into a reflex scheme that is already formed, extending it through the integration of sensori-motor elements hitherto independent of this scheme. Such integration already characterizes Stage 2. Although the child's actions seem to reflect a sort of magical belief in causality without any material contact, his use of the same means to try to achieve different ends indicates that he is on the threshold of intelligence.

3. *Stage 2*

Some such pattern characterizes the formation of the first habits, whether they depend directly upon an activity of the subject, as in the foregoing case, or seem to be imposed from the outside, as in the case of "conditionings." A conditioned reflex is never stabilized by the force of its associations alone, but only by the formation of a scheme of assimilation: that is, when the result attained satisfies the need inherent in the assimilation in question (as with Pavlov's dog, which salivates at the sound of the bell as long as this sound is identified with a signal for food, but which ceases to salivate if food no longer follows the signal).

But even if we use "habits"—for lack of a better word —to refer to acquired behavior while it is being formed as well as after it has become automatized, habit is still not the same as intelligence. An elementary "habit" is based on a general sensori-motor scheme within which there is not yet, from the subject's point of view, any differentiation between means and ends. The end in question is attained only by a necessary succession of movements which lead to it, without one's being able to distinguish either an end pursued from the start or means chosen from among various possible schemes. In an act of intelligence, on the other hand, the end is established from the outset and pursued after a search for the appropriate means. These means are furnished by the schemes known to the subject (or "habit" schemes), but they are used to achieve an aim that had its source in a different scheme.

4. *Stage 3*

The most interesting aspect of the development of sensori-motor actions during the first year of the child's life is that it not only leads to elementary learning experiences which are the source of simple habits on a level where intelligence, strictly speaking, is not yet observed, but it also provides a continuous series of intermediaries between habitual and intelligent reactions. Thus after the reflex stage (Stage 1) and the stage of the first habits (Stage 2), a third stage (Stage 3) introduces the next transitions after the beginning of coordination between vision and prehension—around four and a half months on the average.

The baby starts grasping and manipulating everything he sees in his immediate vicinity. For example, a subject of this age catches hold of a cord hanging from the top of his cradle, which has the effect of shaking all the rattles suspended above him. He immediately repeats the gesture a number of times. Each time the interesting result motivates the repetition. This constitutes a "circular reaction" in the sense of J. M. Baldwin, or a new habit in the nascent state, where the result to be obtained is not differentiated from the means employed. Later you need only hang a new toy from the top of the cradle for the child to look for the cord, which constitutes the beginning of a differentiation between means and end. In the days that follow, when you swing an object from a pole two yards from the crib, and even when you produce unexpected and mechanical sounds behind a screen, after these sights or sounds have ceased the child will again look for and pull the magic cord. Although the child's actions seem to reflect a sort of magical belief in causality without any material connection, his use of the same means to try to achieve different ends indicates that he is on the threshold of intelligence.

5. Stages 4 and 5

In a fourth stage (Stage 4), we observe more complete acts of practical intelligence. The subject sets out to obtain a certain result, independent of the means he is going to employ: for example, obtaining an object that is out of reach or has just disappeared under a piece of cloth or a cushion. The instrumental acts appear only later and they are obviously seen from the outset as means: for example, seizing the hand of an adult and moving it in the direction of the unreachable object, or lifting the screen that masks the hidden object. In the course of this fourth stage, the coordination of means and ends is new and is invented differently in each unforeseen situation (otherwise we would not speak of intelligence), but the means employed are derived only from known schemes of assimilation. (In the case of the object that is hidden and found again, the combination is also new, as we shall see in the next section. But the fact of seizing and moving a cushion corresponds to a habitual scheme.)

In the course of a fifth stage (Stage 5), which makes its appearance around eleven or twelve months, a new ingredient is added to the foregoing behavior: the search for new means by differentiation from schemes already known. An example of this is what we call the "behavior pattern of the support." An object has been placed on a rug out of the child's reach. The child, after trying in vain to reach the object directly, may eventually grasp one corner of the rug (by chance or as a substitute), and then, observing a relationship between the movements of the rug and those of the object, gradually comes to pull the rug in order to reach the object. An analogous discovery characterizes the behavior pattern of the string, studied first by Bühler and then by many others: bringing the objective to oneself by pulling the string to which it is attached.

6. *Stage 6*

Finally, a sixth stage marks the end of the sensori-motor period and the transition to the following period. In this stage the child becomes capable of finding new means not only by external or physical groping but also by internalized combinations that culminate in sudden comprehension or *insight*. For example, a child confronted by a slightly open matchbox containing a thimble first tries to open the box by physical groping (reaction of the fifth stage), but upon failing, he presents an altogether new reaction: he stops the action and attentively examines the situation (in the course of this he slowly opens and closes his mouth, or, as another subject did, his hand, as if in imitation of the result to be attained, that is, the enlargement of the opening), after which he suddenly slips his finger into the crack and thus succeeds in opening the box.

It is at this same stage that one generally finds the well-known behavior pattern of the stick, first studied by Köhler in chimpanzees and later by others in the human infant. But Köhler, like Bühler, considers that there is an act of intelligence involved only in cases where there is sudden comprehension. He banishes groping from the domain of intelligence and classifies it with the behavior of substitution, etc. Claparède, on the other hand, saw groping as the criterion of intelligence, attributing the onset of hypotheses to an externalized groping. This criterion is surely too broad, since groping exists as early as the reflex and the formation of habits. But the criterion of *insight* is certainly too narrow, for it is by means of an uninterrupted succession of assimilations on various levels (Stages 1 through 5) that the sensori-motor schemes lead to those new combinations and internalizations that finally make immediate comprehension possible in certain situations. This last level (Stage 6) cannot therefore be separated from the others; it merely marks their completion.

II. *The Construction of Reality* [5]

The system of sensori-motor schemes of assimilation culminates in a kind of logic of action involving the establishment of relationships and correspondences (functions)
and classification of schemes (cf. the logic of classes); in
short, structures of ordering and assembling that constitute
a substructure for the future operations of thought. But
sensori-motor intelligence has an equally important result
as regards the structuring of the subject's universe, however limited it may be at this practical level. It organizes
reality by constructing the broad categories of action which
are the schemes of the permanent object, space, time, and
causality, substructures of the notions that will later correspond to them. None of these categories is given at the
outset, and the child's initial universe is entirely centered
on his own body and action in an egocentrism as total as
it is unconscious (for lack of consciousness of the self). In
the course of the first eighteen months, however, there occurs a kind of Copernican revolution, or, more simply, a
kind of general decentering process whereby the child
eventually comes to regard himself as an object among
others in a universe that is made up of permanent objects
(that is, structured in a spatio-temporal manner) and in
which there is at work a causality that is both localized in
space and objectified in things.

[5] Jean Piaget, *The Construction of Reality in the Child* (New
York: Basic Books, 1954; London: Routledge and Kegan Paul,
1955).

1. *The Permanent Object*

The first characteristic of this practical universe, which the child builds up during the second year, is that it consists of permanent objects. The universe of the young baby is a world without objects, consisting only of shifting and unsubstantial "tableaux" which appear and are then totally reabsorbed, either without returning, or reappearing in a modified or analogous form. At about five to seven months (Stage 3 of Infancy), when the child is about to seize an object and you cover it with a cloth or move it behind a screen, the child simply withdraws his already extended hand or, in the case of an object of special interest (his bottle, for example), begins to cry or scream with disappointment. He reacts, therefore, as if the object had been reabsorbed. It will perhaps be objected that he knows very well that the object still exists in the place where it has disappeared, but simply does not succeed in solving the problem of looking for it and removing the screen. But when he begins to look under the screen (see Stage 4), you can make the following experiment: hide the object in *A* to the right of the child, who looks for and finds it; then, before his eyes, remove and hide the object in *B*, to the left of the child. When he has seen the object disappear in *B* (under a cushion, say), it often happens that he looks for it in *A*, as if the position of the object depended upon his previous search which was successful rather than upon changes of place which are autonomous and independent of the child's action. In Stage 5 (nine to ten months), however, the object is sought in terms of its displacements alone, unless they are too complex (screens within screens), and in Stage 6 there appears a use of inferences successful in mastering certain combinations (picking up a cushion and finding nothing under it but another unexpected screen, which is then immediately removed).[6]

The conservation of the object is, among other things, a function of its localization; that is, the child simultaneously learns that the object does not cease to exist when it disappears and he learns where it does go. This fact shows from the outset that the formation of the scheme of the permanent object is closely related to the whole spatio-temporal and causal organization of the practical universe.

2. *Space and Time*

To begin with the spatio-temporal structures, we observe that in the beginning there exists neither a single space nor a temporal order which contains objects and events in the same way as containers include their contents. There are, rather, several heterogeneous spaces all centered on the child's own body—buccal, tactile, visual, auditory, and postural spaces—and certain temporal impressions (waiting, etc.), but without objective coordination. These different spaces are then gradually coordinated (buccal and

[6] These results, obtained by one of us, have since been confirmed by Th. Gouin-Décarie in Montreal (in ninety subjects) and by S. Escalona in New York. Escalona has noted that an object hidden in the hand is sought later than one hidden under an external screen (in other words, reabsorption without localization prevails over substantial and spatial permanence for a longer time). H. Gruber has made a study of the same problem in kittens. Kittens pass through approximately the same stages but reach a beginning of permanence as early as three months. The human infant, on this point as on many others, is backward in comparison to the young animal, but this backwardness bears witness to more complex assimilations, since later the human infant is able to go far beyond the animal.

tactilo-kinesthetic, through sucking objects, for instance),
but these coordinations remain partial for a long time, until
the formation of the scheme of the permanent object has
led to the fundamental distinction—which H. Poincaré
wrongly thought was given from the outset [7]—between
changes of state, or physical modifications, and changes
of position, or movements constitutive of space.

Along with the behavior patterns of localization of and
search for the permanent object, the displacements are
finally organized (Stages 5 and 6) into a fundamental
structure which constitutes the framework of practical
space. This structure will later serve as the foundation,
once it has been internalized, for the operations of Euclidean geometry. These displacements form what geometri-
cians call a "group of displacements." Psychologically
speaking, this group has the following characteristics: (a)
A displacement AB and a displacement BC may be coordinated into a single displacement AC, which is still part
of the system.[8] (b) Every displacement AB may be reversed to BA, whence the behavior pattern of "return" to
the point of departure. (c) The combining of the displace-

---

[7] Poincaré had the great merit of foreseeing that the organization of space was related to the formation of the "group of displacements," but since he was not a psychologist, he regarded this
group as *a priori* instead of seeing it as the product of a gradual
formation.

[8] The path AC may not pass through B if AB and BC are not in
a straight line.

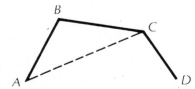

ment AB with its reverse BA gives the null displacement AA. (d) The displacements are associative; that is, in the series $ABCD$, $AB + BD = AC + CD$. This means that by starting from A an identical point D may be reached by different paths (if the segments AB, BC, etc., are not along a straight line). When the child understands this property of space he can begin to solve "detour" problems. It is a late development (Stages 5 and 6 in the human infant) and is an activity understood by chimpanzees but unknown to hens, etc.

This organization of positions and of displacements in space goes together with the constitution of objective temporal series, since, in the case of the practical group of displacements, the displacements are effected physically, step by step, and one at a time, as opposed to the abstract notions which will later be constructed by thought and which will permit a general representation that is simultaneous and increasingly extra-temporal.

3. *Causality*

The system of permanent objects and their displacements is, moreover, indissociable from a causal structuration, for the property of an object is to be the source, the seat, or the result of various actions whose connections constitute the category of causality.

Causality develops in a similar manner as spatio-temporal schemes and becomes objective and adequate only at the end of a long evolution whose initial phases are centered on the child's own action, while he is still unaware of the spatial and physical connections inherent in the material causal schemes. As late as Stage 3, when the infant has already begun smiling at what he sees and manipulating objects according to various schemes (shifting, swinging, striking, rubbing, etc.), he still knows no other cause but his own action, and is not aware of the necessity of spatial contact. In the observation of the cord hanging from the top of the cradle, the baby does not locate the cause of the movement of the dangling rattles in the connection between the cord and the rattles, but rather in the global action of "pulling the cord," which is quite another thing. The proof is that he continues to pull the cord in an attempt to act upon objects situated two yards away, or to act upon sounds, etc. Similarly, other subjects in this third stage arch their bodies and fall back as a means of rocking their cradles, but also to act upon objects at a distance. Later an infant may squint in front of an electric light switch in order to turn on the light, etc.

This early notion of causality may be called magical-phenomenalist: "phenomenalist" because the phenomenal contiguity of two events is sufficient to make them appear causally related, and "magical" because it is centered on the action of the subject without consideration of spatial connection between cause and effect. The first of these two aspects recalls Hume's interpretation of causality, but with exclusive emphasis on the child's own action. The second aspect recalls the conceptions of Maine de Biran, but here there is neither awareness of the ego nor delimitation between self and the outside world.

However, as the universe is increasingly structured by the sensori-motor intelligence according to a spatio-temporal organization and by the formation of permanent objects, causality becomes objectified and spatialized: that is, the subject becomes able to recognize not only the causes situated in his own actions but also in various objects, and the causal relationships between two objects or their actions presuppose a physical and spatial connection. In the behavior patterns of the support, the string, and the stick (Stages 5 and 6), for example, it is clear that the movements of the rug, the string, or the stick are believed to influence those of the object (independently of the author of the displacement), provided there is contact. If the object is placed beside the rug and not on it, the child at Stage 5 will not pull the supporting object, whereas the child at Stage 3 or even 4 who has been trained to make use of the supporting object (or who has discovered its role by accident) will still pull the rug even if the object no longer maintains with it the spatial relationship "placed upon."

III. *The Cognitive Aspect of Sensori-motor Reactions*

If one compares the phases of the construction of reality with those of the construction of the sensori-motor schemes which characterize the functioning of reflexes, habits, or intelligence itself, one observes the existence of a law of development which is of some importance, because it will also govern all the later intellectual development of the child.

The sensori-motor schemes are revealed in three broad successive forms (the preceding ones not disappearing until the following ones appear):

1. The initial forms consist in *rhythm-structures,* such as may be observed in the spontaneous and global movements of the organism, whose reflexes are no doubt merely

gradual differentiations of these movements. The individual reflexes themselves, for that matter, still depend upon a rhythmic structure, not only in their complex arrangements (sucking, locomotion), but because the movements they involve start from an initial state X and proceed to a final stage Z and then begin again in the same order (immediately or at a later time).

2. Next come the various *regulations* that differentiate the initial rhythms according to multiple schemes. The commonest form of these regulations is the control by groping that enters into the formation of the first habits ("circular reactions" insure the transition between rhythm and regulations) and into the first acts of intelligence. These regulations, cybernetic models of which involve loop systems, or feedbacks, thus attain a semi-reversibility, or approximate reversibility, by the retroactive effect of gradual corrections.

3. At last there appears a beginning of *reversibility,* the source of future "operations" of thought, but already functioning at the sensori-motor level as early as the formation of the practical group of displacements (every displacement AB implies a reverse displacement BA). The most immediate result of the reversible structures is the formation of notions of conservation or "group invariants." As early as the sensori-motor level, the reversible organization of the displacements leads to the elaboration of a similar invariant in the form of the scheme of the permanent object. But it is obvious that on the sensori-motor level neither this reversibility in action nor this conservation is yet complete, for lack of mental representation.

If the rhythmic structures no longer appear at the later representative levels (from two to fifteen years), the whole evolution of thought will be dominated, as we shall see presently, by a general transition from regulations to an internalized or operatory reversibility; that is, reversibility in the strict sense of the term.

IV. *The Affective Aspect of Sensori-motor Reactions*

When behavior is studied in its cognitive aspect, we are concerned with its structures; when behavior is considered in its affective aspect, we are concerned with its energetics (or "economics," as Pierre Janet used to say). While these two aspects cannot be reduced to a single aspect, they are nevertheless inseparable and complementary. For this reason we must not be surprised to find a marked parallelism in their respective evolutions. The cognitive schemes which are initially centered upon the child's own action become the means by which the child constructs an objective and "decentered" universe; similarly, and at the same sensori-motor levels, affectivity proceeds from a lack of differentiation between the self and the physical and human environment toward the construction of a group of exchanges or emotional investments which attach the differentiated self to other persons (through interpersonal feelings) or things (through interests at various levels).

Studying the infant's affectivity is much more difficult than studying his cognitive functions, however, for the risk of "adultomorphism" is much greater in this area. Most of the well-known studies are psychoanalytically oriented and for a long time were limited to the reconstruction of the early stages in the emotional life of the child in terms of adult psychopathology. R. Spitz, K. Wolf, and Th. Gouin-Décarie, however, have adopted experimental procedures to assist in the psychoanalysis of the baby, and the current research of S. Escalona, whose inspiration is both psychoanalytic and Lewinian, is breaking out of the limitations of the Freudian definitions and reaching the level of objective analysis and control.

1. *The Initial Adualism*

The affects peculiar to the first two stages (Stages 1 and 2 of infancy) occur within a context already described by Baldwin under the name of "adualism," in which there does not yet exist any consciousness of the self; that is, any boundary between the internal or experienced world and the world of external realities. Freud talked about narcissism but did not sufficiently stress the fact that this was narcissism without a Narcissus. Anna Freud has since clarified the concept of "primary narcissism" as an initial lack of differentiation between the self and the other. H. Wallon describes this same undifferentiation in terms of symbiosis. Insofar as the self remains undifferentiated, and thus unconscious of itself, all affectivity is centered on the child's own body and action, since only with the dissociation of the self from the other or non-self does decentration, whether affective or cognitive, become possible. The root notion contained in the term "narcissism" is valid provided we make it clear that an unconscious centering due to undifferentiation is not at all like a conscious centering of one's emotional life upon the self which can occur in later life.

The affects observable in this adualistic period are at first dependent upon general rhythms corresponding to the rhythms of the spontaneous global activities of the organism; namely, alternations between states of tension and relaxation, etc. These rhythms are differentiated into a search for agreeable stimuli and a tendency to avoid disagreeable stimuli.

The most frequently studied symptom of satisfaction is the smile. Charlotte Bühler believed the smile was a specific reaction to the human person, but there is reason to doubt this interpretation. In the first place, newborn babies exhibit, soon after feeding, a kind of physiological smile, without any visual stimulus. In the second place, some very precocious smiles have been observed in the presence of moving objects. The most convincing evidence, however, comes from studies made with more or less complete masks (eyes and forehead without mouth, etc.) like the "dummies" used by Tinbergen and Lorenz to analyze the perceptual triggers of innate mechanisms. Here it has been observed that the eyes and the upper part of the face play a predominant role. Certain writers, such as J. Bowlby, regard these stimuli as hereditary triggers (IRM).[9] But Spitz[10] and Wolf see the smile simply as a sign of the recognition of a complex of stimuli in a context of need satisfaction, and we tend to agree with their position. According to this view, there is no initial recognition of the face as a person, but since the infant's smile is very frequently provoked, maintained, reinforced, or "gratified" by the smile of the human partner, it becomes an instrument of exchange or contagion. Consequently, little by little, it becomes a means of differentiating persons from

[9] Innate releasing mechanisms.
[10] R. Spitz and W. Cobliner, *The First Year of Life* (New York: International Universities Press, 1966).

things (the former being for a long time merely those particularly active and unexpected centers assimilated in
terms of the child's own reactions, without clear differentiation from things).

2. *Intermediary Reactions*

In the course of Stages 3 and 4 we witness, in conjunction with the growing complexity of behavior, an increased
number of psychological satisfactions supplementing organic satisfactions. But these new differentiations are not
uniformly satisfying. We also observe discomfort in the
presence of the unknown, anxieties in the presence of persons who are strangers to the milieu (R. Spitz), reactions to
the strangeness of situations (R. Meili), etc., and also the
beginnings of a tolerance to stress; this tolerance is greater
if the conflict occurs in a situation where contact is otherwise felt as pleasant.

Contact with persons thus becomes more and more important, heralding a transition from contagion to communication (Escalona). Even before the formation of a self
complementary to and interacting with others we witness
the elaboration of a whole system of exchanges through
imitation and the reading of gestural signs. From this time
on, the child begins to react to persons in a more and more
specific manner because they behave differently from
things and because they behave according to schemes
which bear some relation to the schemes of the child's own
action. Sooner or later there is established a kind of causality whose source is others, inasmuch as they produce
pleasure, comfort, pacification, security, etc.

However, it is essential to understand that the totality of
these affective advances is inseparable from the general

structuration of behavior. "My data," concludes Escalona, "suggest the possibility that what Piaget proposes for cognition is true of all adaptive aspects of mental functioning: namely, that the emergence of such functions as communication, modulation of affect, control over excitation, delay, and aspects of object relation, and hence identification, all are the result of a developmental sequence in sensori-motor terms, before they can emerge as ego functions in the narrower sense." [11]

3. *"Object" Relations*

In the course of Stages 5 and 6 (with preparation as early as Stage 4), we witness something which Freud called a "choice of the [affective] object" and which he regarded as a transference of "libido" from the narcissistic self onto the person of the parents. Psychoanalysts today talk about "object relations," and ever since Hartmann and Rapaport insisted on the autonomy of the ego in relation to the libido, they conceive the appearance of these object relations as marking the double formation of a self differentiated from other people and other people becoming objects of affectivity. Baldwin had already long since insisted on the role of imitation in the development of the self, which attests to the interdependent and complementary nature of the formation of the *ego* and the *alter*.

The problems, then, are to understand why this decentering of affectivity onto the person of the other occurs at this level of development, and above all to understand

[11] Sibylle Escalona, "Patterns of Infantile Experience and the Developmental Process," in R. Eissler et al., eds., *The Psychoanalytic Study of the Child* (New York: International Universities Press, 1963), Vol. 18, pp. 198–199.

how this decentering takes place. We have assumed that affective decentering is a correlative of cognitive decentering, not because one dominates the other, but because both occur as a result of a single integrated process. Indeed, when the little child ceases to relate everything to his states and to his own action, and begins to substitute for a world of fluctuating tableaux without spatio-temporal consistency or external physical causality a universe of permanent objects structured according to its own groups of spatio-temporal displacements and according to an objectified and spatialized causality, then his affectivity will also be attached to these localizable permanent objects and sources of external causality which persons come to be. Whence the formation of "object relations" in close connection with the scheme of permanent objects.

This hypothesis, which is very plausible but not self-evident, has been verified by Gouin-Décarie.[12] As mentioned in Section II (page 15), Gouin-Décarie examined the regular evolution of the stages in the formation of the scheme of the object in ninety subjects. In the same subjects she analyzed affective reactions in terms of a scale based on "object relations" (the evolution thus observed is clear, although less regular than that of cognitive reactions). With these two kinds of data, Gouin-Décarie was able to show the existence of a significant correlation[13] in which the stages of affectivity corresponded broadly to

[12] Th. Gouin-Décarie, *Intelligence et affectivité chez le jeune enfant* (Neuchâtel: Delachaux et Niestlé, 1962).

[13] Similarly, E. J. Anthony has shown the existence of lacunae in the scheme of the permanent object in psychotic children showing disturbances in object relations. See "Six Applications de la théorie génétique de Piaget à la théorie et à la pratique psychodynamique," *Revue suisse de psychologie,* Vol. XV (1956).

those of the construction of the object for each group of subjects.[14]

As a final comment we should note that these various correlations between cognitive development and interpersonal interactions tend to modify the conclusions to be drawn from children's reactions to institutionalization. The psychoanalysts Spitz, Bowlby, and others have studied the effects of separation from the mother in charitable institutions. The facts gathered have shown the existence of systematic (and, it should be added, elective) retardations in development and even of arrests and regressions in cases of permanent separation. But here again it is necessary to consider all the factors. It is not necessarily the maternal element as affectively specialized (in the Freudian sense) that plays the principal role, but the lack of stimulating interactions; but these may be associated with the mother insofar as she creates a private mode of exchange between a given adult with her character and a given child with his.

[14] It remains to be noted that, insofar as such correlations are verified, that is, insofar as affectivity is inseparable from the whole of behavior without constituting either a cause or an effect of the cognitive structurations, the essential factor in object relations is the relation itself between the subject and the affective object; that is, the interaction between them, and not essentially the factor "mother" functioning as an independent variable, as neo-Freudian psychoanalysis continues to assume. As has been shown by S. Escalona, whose acute observations of individual and differential psychology have led her to a more relativist position, the same maternal partner provokes different results according to the general behavior of the child, just as different children touch off distinct reactions in the same mother.

B*

2

THE DEVELOPMENT
OF PERCEPTION

As REGARDS THE DEVELOPMENT of the cognitive functions in the child, Chapter 1 has suggested, and the following chapters will confirm, that the sensori-motor structures constitute the source of the later operations of thought. This means that intelligence proceeds from action as a whole, in that it transforms objects and reality, and that knowledge, whose formation can be traced in the child, is essentially an active and operatory assimilation.

However, the empiricist tradition, which has had so much influence on a certain branch of pedagogy, regards knowledge as a kind of copy of reality and intelligence as deriving from perception alone (the term "sensation" is no longer used in this sense). Even the great Leibniz, who defended intelligence against sensualism (adding *nisi ipse intellectus* to the adage *nil est in intellectu quod non prius fuerit in sensu*), accepted the idea that even if the forms of notions, judgments, and arguments are not derived from the "senses," their content does stem wholly from that source. As if there were nothing more in mental life than sensations and reason—forgetting action!

To understand the child's development, therefore, it is necessary to examine the evolution of his perceptions in the light of the role of the sensori-motor structures. Indeed, perception constitutes a special case of sensori-motor activity. But its special character consists in the fact that it pictures reality in its figurative aspect whereas an action as a whole (and even sensori-motor action) is essentially operative and transforms the real. It is important, therefore, to determine the relative roles of perceptions and actions (and later operations) in the intellectual development of the child.

I. *Perceptual Constancies and Perceptual Causality*

It would be appropriate to begin our analysis with a study of the perceptions of the newborn child and to follow them throughout the sensori-motor period. Unfortunately, however, nothing is more difficult to study than the perceptions of the young infant, since we are unable to subject the baby to precise laboratory experiments. It is true that we possess some neurological information on the development of the sense organs,[1] but this is by no means ade-

---

[1] According to W. E. Hunt, electroretinograms show that a few hours after birth retinal receptors are already capable of functioning (myelin is not necessary to functioning, but serves to isolate

quate for reconstructing the nature of the perceptions themselves. On the other hand, two famous problems of perception can be examined in relation to the sensori-motor reactions of the first year: that of constancy and that of perceptual causality.

Constancy of size refers to the maintenance in perception of the real size of an object viewed from a distance, regardless of its apparent shrinking. Constancy of form is the perception of the habitual form of an object (that is, as seen from the frontal parallel plane), regardless of its perspective presentation. These two perceptual constancies make their appearance in an approximate form by the second half of the first year, and then become refined until the age of ten to twelve or even later.[2] The question therefore arises as to their relationship to the sensori-motor schemes, notably that of the permanent object.

---

the axons and corresponds to more mature electrophysiological reactions). According to A. H. Keeney, postnatal development of the fovea and the pericentral area is very rapid during the first four months. After that there is a gradual change until adolescence: in particular, stratification of the cones increases from a single layer at birth to three layers at sixteen weeks, the maximum depth of four or five being achieved only at adolescence.

According to J. L. Conel, during a good part of childhood the region of the occipital lobes, which receives a high proportion of fibers from the macula, is less well developed in all respects than the regions receiving their fibers from the periphery of the retina. According to P. I. Yakolov, the quantity of myelin along the nervous tracts increases until the age of sixteen.

[2] Not to mention "overconstancy" of size, or overestimation of the height of distant objects, which makes its appearance at eight or nine and is rather widespread in adults.

1. *Constancy of Form*

One of us[3] has observed a relationship between certain constancies of form and the permanence of the object. When he handed a baby of seven or eight months its bottle backwards, he observed that the infant turned the bottle around easily if it noticed part of the red rubber nipple in the background, but that it did not succeed in making this correction if it did not see any part of the nipple and only the white base of the milk-filled bottle was visible. This child, then, did not attribute a constant form to the bottle. However, as soon as he began to look for objects behind screens (at the age of nine months), he readily turned the bottle around no matter how it was presented, as if the permanence of the object and the constant form of the object were related. One can assume that in this case an interaction occurs between perception and the sensori-motor scheme, for the first is not sufficient to explain the second (the search for an object that has disappeared is not dependent on its shape alone), nor the second sufficient to explain the first.

2. *Constancy of Size*

Constancy of size makes its appearance at about six months. Once the child has been trained to choose the larger of two boxes, he continues to choose correctly if you move the larger box farther away, so that its retinal image is smaller (E. Brunswik and R. M. Cruikshank). Hence this constancy makes its appearance before the formation of the permanent object but after the coordination of vision

[3] Jean Piaget, *The Mechanisms of Perception* (New York: Basic Books, 1969; London: Routledge and Kegan Paul, 1969).

and prehension (at about four and a half months). This last fact is of some importance, for it may be wondered why a perceptual constancy of size exists for near objects but disappears for distant ones, when intelligence alone determines the real size of elements that have apparently shrunk. The answer is no doubt that the size of an object is variable to the sight but constant to the touch, and that the whole sensori-motor development imposes a coordination between the visual and the tactilo-kinesthetic sensations. It is no accident, then, that constancy of size makes its appearance after and not before the coordination of vision and prehension; although of a perceptual nature, constancy thus depends upon the overall sensori-motor schemes. (And if it can later further the permanence of the object, constancy of size will in turn be improved, once this permanence has been acquired.)

3. *The Permanent Object and Perception*

These first two examples tend, therefore, to demonstrate the irreducibility of the sensori-motor to the perceptive, since both cases suggest that perception renders indispensable services to sensori-motor activity, but that it is reciprocally enriched by this activity. Neither can totally explain the other. Attempts have nevertheless been made to account for the formation of the permanent object by perceptual factors. For example, Michotte sees object permanence as the product of perceptual effects which he calls the "screen effect" (for instance, an object A passing under another object B is recognized, even though A is partly hidden, by the organization of the boundaries according to the laws that govern figure and background) and the "tunnel effect" (that is, even though *A* completely disappears while passing under *B,* if its speed is perceived before its entrance, one has a perceptual but not a sensory impression of its positions and anticipates its exit). The question, however, is whether or not "screen" and "tunnel" effects are present in the baby before the formation of the permanent object. Experiment shows that the "tunnel effect" is not. Suppose you show a child a moving object following a course *ABCD.* It appears from under a screen at *A,* is visible from *A* to *B,* is hidden by a screen from *B* to *C,* is visible from *C* to *D* and finally disappears again at *D.* A child of five to six months follows the path *AB* with his eyes and, when the object disappears at *B,* looks for it at *A*; then, amazed to see it at *C,* he follows it with his eyes from *C* to *D,* but when the object disappears at *D,* looks for it at *C* and then at *A*! In other words, there is no "tunnel effect" at that age; in fact, it does not appear until the permanence of the object has been established. In this case a perceptual effect is clearly determined by sensori-motor schemes, rather than explaining them.

4. *Perceptual Causality*

Finally, Michotte's well-known experiments in perceptual causality should be mentioned. When a little square *A,* set in motion, touches a motionless square *B* and *B* moves (*A* remaining motionless after the impact), one has a perceptual impression that *A pushed B,* depending on the precise conditions of speed and spatial or temporal relations (if *B* does not move immediately, the causal impression disappears and the movement of *B* appears to be independent). Similarly, one has impressions of *pulling* (if *A* continues its course behind *B* after the impact) and of *launching* (if the speed of *B* is greater than that of *A*).

Michotte has tried to explain sensori-motor causality by way of perceptual causality, conceived as more primitive; but this explanation encounters several difficulties. The main difficulty is that until about the age of seven years the child recognizes "launching" only if he has noticed contact between *A* and *B*, whereas subjects between seven and twelve and adults have an impression of "launching at a distance" if there is a perceived interval of two to three millimeters between *A* and *B*. But the sensori-motor notion of causality which we have called "magical-phenomenalist" (page 18) is by its very nature independent of all spatial contact. It cannot be derived from perceptual causality since the child's perception of causality is more dependent on the conditions of impact than the adult's, but his beliefs about causality are less so.[4]

---

[4] Moreover, visual perceptual causality is characterized by impressions of impact, thrust, resistance, weight, etc. (when square *B* moves more slowly than square *A*, it appears "heavier" and more resistant than when it moves at the same speed), which are in no way actually visual. In this case as in many others, therefore, it is a question of impressions that are tactilo-kinesthetic in origin but are later translated into corresponding visual terms. Indeed, there exists a tactilo-kinesthetic perceptual causality which Michotte himself regards as genetically anterior to visual causality. But this tactilo-kinesthetic perceptual causality depends upon action as a whole. The only causality known in a tactile manner derives from thrusting actions, etc., which the child experiences as performed by his own body. It seems evident here too that it is the sensori-motor schematism which determines the perceptual mechanisms, rather than the reverse.

II. *Field Effects*

If we now consider perceptions between the ages of about four to about fifteen, that is, from the age at which laboratory experiments become possible, two kinds of visual perceptual phenomena can be distinguished: (1) Field effects, or centering effects, which do not involve any eye movements and which exist in a single field of focus (these can be studied by tachistoscopic presentation which exposes a stimulus for such a short duration [.05 to .20 seconds] that there cannot be any change of focus); and (2) perceptual activities involving movements of the gaze in space, or comparisons of two stimuli appearing in the same place but at different times (both oriented by an active search on the part of the subject), exploration, transfer (of what is seen at X to what is seen at Y) in space or in time, transposition of a whole body of relationships, anticipations and comparisons of directions, etc.

Of course, perceptual activities develop with age both in number and in quality. A child of nine or ten makes use of references and directions (perceptual coordinates) that are overlooked at five or six; he explores figures more thoroughly, anticipates more often, etc. In principle, perceptual activities improve perception and correct the systematic "illusions" or distortions peculiar to field effects. But in creating new relationships, they may give rise to new systematic errors, which then increase with age (at least up to a certain point).[5]

[5] For example, the so-called size-weight illusion: when two boxes of equal weight but different volume are compared, the

Field effects remain qualitatively the same at every age, except that sooner or later new ones may be formed *as perceptual activity changes*. They provide perceptions that are approximately adequate, but only approximately, because immediate perception is the product of a sampling of a probabilistic nature. In looking at a configuration, even a very simple one, only a small area can be clearly seen in each single glance. One does not in fact see everything with the same precision, and one does not see everything at the same time. The gaze moves from one point to another, and the "encounters" between the different parts of the receptive organs and the different parts of the stimulus object are distributed with unequal density according to the regions of the figure, the regions of the retina, and whether at a given moment these regions are centered by the fovea (zone of clear vision) or remain in the periphery (perifoveal zone). The result is that field effects, although roughly adequate, are always partially distorting. These systematic "illusions" or distortions remain qualitatively the same at every age, but diminish in intensity or in their quantitative value as the child grows older and they are to a certain degree corrected by perceptual activities (exploration, etc.).

If "primary" optico-geometric illusions (arising from

---

larger box appears lighter by contrast in proportion as the subject expects it to be heavier. This perceptual error is greater at ten to twelve than it is at five or six, because anticipation is more active. Extremely backward children, who anticipate nothing, do not experience this illusion. Binet also made this distinction between the illusions that increase with age and those that decrease. As a matter of fact, the former all depend indirectly upon perceptual activities, whereas the latter depend upon field effects.

field effects) do not vary qualitatively with age, then the distribution of the illusion, in terms of variations in the figure, notably its positive and negative *maxima,* retains the same properties at every age. For example, in the perception of a rectangle (in which the diagonals are not drawn) one tends to overestimate the long sides and underestimate the short sides. If you vary the short side and leave the long sides constant, the illusion gains in strength as the short sides get shorter; the *maximum* appears when the rectangle merges with the thinnest straight line that can be drawn. In the illusion of the concentric circles (Delboeuf), the small circle is overestimated and the large one underestimated; the positive *maximum* is reached when the radii are in a ratio of three to four. If the small circle has a diameter shorter than the width of the band separating the two circles, the illusion is reversed (underestimation of the small circle) and presents a negative *maximum* for a given ratio. The positions of these *maxima* are the same at every age. So is the median point of no illusion dividing positive from negative errors. On the other hand, and independently of the permanence of these qualitative properties, the quantitative value of the illusion diminishes with age. For the same figure presenting the same *maximum* at every age (for example, Delboeuf's illusion in a three-to-four ratio), the illusion is stronger at the age of five than it is later, and in the adult it reaches no more than half or one-third of its initial value.

These facts are worth mentioning, for they provide a rare example of a reaction that with development varies only in intensity. It is of course impossible to know what happens during the first months of life, but since the illusion of the concentric circles is found even in minnows, it must be rather precocious in the human young.[6]

The duality of factors represented by the number of "encounters" and by complete or incomplete "couplings" may be explained by the *temporal maximum* of illusions, in which one does find some differences with age. If you present a figure for a very short period of time, varying from one or two hundredths of a second to one second, the illusion generally reaches a *maximum* at about one to three tenths of a second. Within the shortest exposure there are

[6] This identity of reactions is due to the simplicity of the probabilistic mechanism that underlies these perceptual distortions. As one of us has shown, it is possible to reduce all primary illusions (field effects) to centering effects, since elements centered by the gaze (fovea) are overestimated and elements situated in the periphery of the visual field are underestimated. This heterogeneity of the visual field results, even if the gaze moves about (exploration), in a heterogeneity of "encounters" with the object in the sense just indicated, since the centerings are not equally distributed and since each centering involves a local overestimation, depending upon the number of encounters. Let us use the word "couplings" to refer to the correspondences l to n between encounters with one element of the figure and encounters with another element. There will be no distortion or illusion if the couplings are complete (and therefore the encounters homogeneous), as in the case of "good forms" like the square, all of whose elements are equal. On the other hand, there will be illusion if the couplings are incomplete, which is favored by the inequalities of length already mentioned. It is possible to calculate the distribution of the illusion (*maxima,* etc.) by means of a simple formula based on the differences in length between the elements of the figure:

$$P \text{ (distortion)} = \frac{(L_1 - L_2) \, L_2}{S} \times \frac{L_1}{L_{\max}},$$

L_1 being the greatest of the two lengths being compared, L_2 being the smallest, $L_{\max}$ being the greatest length of the figure, and S being the surface, or total of possible couplings.

very few encounters, which increases the probability of fairly complete couplings and gives rise to a slight illusion. At durations of from three to five tenths of a second to one second, it becomes possible to shift the gaze and explore more thoroughly. Encounters become numerous, the couplings again become relatively complete, and the illusion decreases. But between the two the encounters increase without the possibility of systematic exploration; therefore the probability of incomplete couplings is greater; whence the *temporal* (and no longer spatial) *maximum* of illusion. Since the *temporal maximum* depends upon the rapidity of the reactions and the quality of the exploration, however, it varies somewhat with age, in contrast to the *spatial maximum,* and sometimes appears in the young child for slightly longer durations than in older children and adults.

III. *The Perceptual Activities*

We have seen that whereas field effects remain relatively constant with age, perceptual activities develop progressively. This is the case with the most important among them: the exploration of configurations by systematic eye movements, shifting one's fixation point in a systematic way. One of us studied with Vinh-Bang (by recording on film) the comparison of two horizontal, oblique, or vertical lines laid end to end, or of the vertical and horizontal lines of an L-shaped figure (the assignment being to judge whether the lines were equal in length or not). There were two clear-cut differences between the reactions of six-year-olds and those of older subjects. First, in the child the points of fixation are much less accurate and are distributed over

a much larger area than in the adult (up to several centimeters from the lines in question). Second, the movements of transfer and of comparison made in scanning
back and forth from one segment to the other are propor-
tionally less frequent in children than simple displacements
of a random appearance. In short, the young subjects
behave as if they were expecting to see everything, even
with aberrant centerings, whereas the adults look more
actively, directing their exploration by means of a strategy
whereby the shifts of fixation obtain a *maximum* of information with a *minimum* of loss.[7]

But the exploration may be too concentrated on special
points and thereby give rise to secondary errors. This is the
case in the horizontal-vertical illusion—vertical lines are
overestimated in relation to horizontal lines of the same
length—because the most frequent centerings cluster
around the middle of the horizontal lines and the top of
the vertical lines (a fact which is confirmed by the recording of eye movements). This error of the vertical tends to
increase with age.

[7] This absence of active exploration explains a characteristic
that has been classically ascribed to the perceptions of children
under seven years of age: namely, their syncretism (Claparède) or
global character (Decroly), which is such that in a complex configuration the subject perceives only the total impression, without
analysis of the parts or synthesis of their relations. G. Meili-Dwor-
etskii, for example, has used an ambiguous figure that can be perceived either as a pair of scissors or as a human face. In adults, the
two configurations present themselves alternately and cannot be
seen simultaneously, since the same circles represent either eyes or
the finger holes of scissors. Yet a number of young subjects said:
"It's a man and somebody threw a pair of scissors in his face."
This syncretism is not predictable and does not derive from field
effects: it simply expresses a lack of systematic exploratory activity.

Moreover, exploration may be combined with effects of exercise and with temporal transfers when the same figure is observed twenty times or more in succession. Here one observes very significant differences with age. These have been established by G. Noelting under the direction of one of us with the Müller-Lyer illusion (the effects of arrow-heads at the end of a line on its apparent length) and the illusion of the rhombus (underestimation of the long diagonal). In the adult, repetition of the experiment leads to a gradual reduction of the systematic error and may even result in its complete elimination. This effect of exercise or of cumulative exploration is all the more interesting in that the subject does not know whether his answers are correct. The influence of external reinforcements is therefore ruled out, and one is led to attribute this form of learning to a gradual equilibration (increasingly complete "couplings"). In the child of seven to twelve the same effects are found; they are weaker in the younger subjects and increase steadily with age. However, with this technique it has not been possible to discover any influence of exercise or repetition in subjects under the age of seven. In these subjects the curve of errors stays at around the same average after twenty, thirty, or even forty repetitions. (There is less fatigue because these subjects do not give evidence of any active exploration.) It is of some interest to note that learning does not make its appearance until around seven. At that age syncretism declines sharply and eye movements are better controlled. Above all, the first logico-mathematical operations appear: perceptual activity can be directed by an intelligence that has a better grasp of the problems. Not, of course, that intelligence at this stage replaces perception, but by structuring reality it helps to program the way perceptual data are collected; that is, it helps indicate where to concentrate the attention. Even in simple linear comparisons, this programming plays an important role, substituting a science of measurement for global or simply ordinal evaluations (see Chapter 4, pages 106–107).

The orienting influence of intelligence is even clearer in the child's use of perceptual coordinates, where reference to horizontal and vertical axes can help him judge the direction of figures or lines. At the request of one of us, H. Wirsten studied the comparison of the length of a vertical line five centimeters long with the length of a variable oblique line (including the horizontal position) whose point of origin was five centimeters from the first line. This comparison is difficult for the adult, who makes considerable errors. It is much easier at five and six, because children pay no attention to the orientation of the lines. (The proof is that the children make a *maximum* of errors in discriminating between different angles of orientation the estimation of which is easy for the adult.) After the age of five or six, errors in judging length become greater, until the age of nine or ten, when they reach a *maximum* and then decrease slightly (as a result of new perceptual activities involving the transfer of lengths, regardless of direction). It is from nine to ten that, in the realm of intelligence, the system of operatory coordinates is being organized and the subject is beginning to notice directions, which distracts him in the perceptual evaluation of lengths.[8]

[8] P. Dadsetan later completed the preceding experiment by having subjects judge the horizontality of a straight line drawn within a triangle whose base was oblique, the whole appearing on a large blank sheet of paper whose edges had been reinforced with black lines to facilitate reference. Without going into detail, we

Generally speaking, then, we see that perceptual activities develop with age until they are able to obey the directives of the intelligence. But before the operations of thought are formed, it is the global action which performs the role of orientation. It is out of the question, therefore, to regard perceptual activities as the result of a simple extension or a simple refinement of field effects, as is suggested by Gestalt theory. On the contrary, it is the field effects that appear to be local consequences of perceptual activities on various levels, for orientations or comparisons of a global nature make their appearance in the very first weeks of life.

IV. *Perceptions, Concepts, and Operations*

Having established these facts, we can now return to the problem raised in the introduction to this chapter: Is the development of perception sufficient to explain the development of intelligence or at least of its content (concepts,

---

would like to point out that the results confirmed previous findings. It is at about nine or ten that the child becomes aware of references external to the triangle. It is at that point that, under the influence of the nascent operatory coordinates, it occurs to him to look at the edges of the sheet of paper, at last going beyond the boundaries of the triangular figure. Moreover, in testing the capacity of the same subjects to use operatory coordinates (by asking them to predict the line of the surface of the water in a jar when it is tilted: see Chapter 3, page 67), Dadsetan found a slight advance in operatory coordination over his perception test, which demonstrates once again the role of intelligence in the programming of perceptual activity.

for example that of perspective), or has sensualism simply forgotten the role of action with its sensori-motor schematism, which may constitute both the source of the perceptions and the basis for the later operations of thought?

1. *Methods*

As far as concepts are concerned, the minimal thesis of empiricism is that their content is derived from perception and that their form consists merely of abstractions and generalizations from experience without any constructive structuration; that is, with no source of connections apart from or superior to the relations provided by perception. We shall observe, on the contrary, that such a structuration is always present and stems from action or from operations. Moreover, it enriches concepts with non-perceptual content (in addition, naturally, to information derived from perception), because from the very beginning the sensori-motor schematism goes beyond perception and is not itself perceptible.

To clarify the problem, we shall choose a number of concepts whose pre-operatory and operatory development is well known and analyze the corresponding perceptions (for example, the perception of speed and the concept of speed, etc.) in order to determine whether the perceptions are sufficient to account for the concepts.

Four kinds of situations are encountered. In the first (Situation 1), perception and concept (or preconcept) appear at the same time, at a level where the concept still consists of a sensori-motor scheme and is not yet representative. We have just seen examples of these relations (permanent object and perceptual constancies or tunnel effect, sensori-motor causality and perceptual causality), which are in this case relations of interaction in which the sensori-motor scheme cannot be reduced to the corresponding perceptual structures.

In Situations 2 through 4 the perceptions precede the corresponding concepts by a long period; these concepts have now become representative.

2. *Projective Concepts and Perceptions*

In Situation 2 there is a divergent evolution between concept and perception. The concepts and representations of perspective (diminution at a distance, receding lines, etc.) do not appear until after the age of seven, when the child can comprehend apparent changes in size or shape according to the viewing point and can represent perspective in drawing. This development reaches a plateau at age nine to ten when the child can coordinate different viewing points in relation to a group of three objects. On the other hand, perception of projective or apparent sizes is very difficult for the adult (judging which one of a series of rods of different lengths situated at a distance of 4 m. corresponds in apparent size to one of 10 cm. at a distance of 1 m.; in fact, a rod of 40 cm. should be chosen). The average adult chooses a rod of about 20 cm., at 4 m., whereas the child of six or seven has a great deal of difficulty understanding the problem, but, once he has understood it, he judges more accurately. After this age, the perception deteriorates, whereas the concept develops—proof in itself that the concept is not simply derived from the perception. Indeed, in this realm perception provides only instant impressions corresponding to a given viewing point (that of the subject at a given moment), whereas the concept presupposes a coordination of all viewing points and an understanding of the transformations leading from one viewing point to another.

3. *Perceptual Constancies and Operatory Conservations*

In Situation 3 there is, on the contrary, a partial isomorphism between the development of perceptions and that of the corresponding concepts. Consequently, perception prefigures concept, as Michotte aptly puts it. But the term "prefiguration" can be used in two quite distinct senses. It can mean that perception is the direct precursor of the concept, and this is what Michotte, whose Gestaltist and Aristotelian commitments are well known, had in mind. Or it can mean that perception and concept are constructed analogously, with collateral rather than causal relationships, the common source being the sensori-motor schematism.

An example of these simple prefigurations is the relation between the perceptual constancies that we have already discussed (pages 29 ff.) and the operatory conservations that we shall examine later on (Chapter 4). Both processes, in fact, consist in recognizing the invariance of some property of the object: its real size or shape, in the case of the perceptual constancies, when its apparent size or shape is modified; its quantity of matter, weight, etc., in the case of the operatory conservations, for example, when a liquid is poured from one container to another or the shape of a lump of clay is changed. Both conservation and perceptual constancy, moreover, are based on mechanisms of compensation by multiplicative composition (in the logical sense of the term). In the case of size constancy, the retinal size decreases as the distance increases, and the real size is perceived as approximately constant through the coordination of these two variables. In the case of the conservation of matter, the child judges the quantity of liquid to be permanent when he sees that although the level of the liquid rises in a thinner glass, the width of the column decreases. As a consequence, the amount of liquid remains constant by compensation (logical or deductive compensation, obviously, without any measurement or numerical calculation). Hence there is a structural analogy or partial isomorphism between the mechanisms of constancy and of conservation.

However, the first operatory conservations do not make their appearance until around seven or eight (substance) and others are added at intervals until the age of twelve (volume). In fact, the mechanism of deductive compensation is absent until the age of six or seven. On the other hand, the perceptual constancies appear during the first year (sensori-motor period). It is true that they continue to develop until about the age of ten: subjects of five to seven slightly underestimate sizes at a distance, whereas older children and adults overestimate them (overconstancy by excess of compensation), but the mechanism of perceptual compensations functions as early as six to twelve months, nearly seven years before operatory compensations.

In order to make a judgment about the genetic kinship or possible direct linear relation between constancies and conservations, it is necessary to explain this time lag. The explanation is simple. In the case of perceptual constancies, the object is not changed in reality, only in appearance; that is, only from the viewing point of the subject. There is no need to reason to correct the appearance; a perceptual regulation is sufficient (whence the approximate character of the constancies and the hyperregulations resulting in overconstancies). In the case of the conservations, however, the object is modified in reality, and to understand in what respect it is invariant it is necessary to construct operationally a system of transformations providing for the compensations.

In conclusion, the fact that constancies and conservations develop in an analogous fashion by regulatory or operatory compensation does not mean that the latter are derived from the former, given their far greater complexity. There is a relation, but a collateral one: the operatory conservations constitute a direct extension of the early recognition of invariance, namely the scheme of the permanent object (early because the object is not then modified and is merely moved from one place to another as in the case of the constancies, although completely leaving the perceptual field). And, as we have seen, interactions do exist between the scheme and the nascent constancies.

4. *Situation 4*

Situation 4 presents prefigurations analogous to Situations 2 and 3, except that in the later stages intelligence itself influences perception.[9]

[9] An example of this would be the perceptual coordinates already discussed. Here there is prefiguration of the concept in the perception, in the sense that at all perceptual levels certain directions are evaluated in terms of references (the child's own body or elements close to the object under consideration), but once the operatory coordinates have been established as generalized operations of measurement in two or three dimensions, they then influence perception, as we have seen.

5. *Conclusion*

Generally speaking, it is therefore impossible to maintain that the concepts of intelligent thought are simply derived from the perceptions through abstraction and generalization. In addition to perceptual data, concepts incorporate specific constructions of a more or less complex nature. Logico-mathematical concepts presuppose a set of operations that are abstracted not from the objects perceived but from the actions performed on these objects, which is by no means the same. Even if every action can give rise to exteroceptive and proprioceptive perceptions, the schemes of these actions are no longer perceptible. In the case of physical concepts, etc., the proportion of perceptual information necessary is greater. However elementary they may be in the child, these concepts cannot be elaborated without a logico-mathematical structuration that, once again, goes beyond perception.

Let us now turn briefly to the operations themselves, which will be discussed more fully in Chapters 4 and 5. Max Wertheimer, one of the originators of Gestalt theory, has attempted to reduce them to perceptual structure.[10] Gestaltism, as we know, interprets all intelligence as an extension, to wider and wider areas, of the "forms" initially governing the world of perceptions. What we have just said in the preceding pages, however, contradicts such an interpretation. Moreover, as far as the operations themselves are concerned, there are the following considerations. The perceptual structures are essentially irreversible because they are based on a probabilistic mode of composition

[10] *Productive Thinking* (New York: Harper, 1945).

which is obvious in the realm of field effects but which still influences the regulations characteristic of perceptual activities (although these regulations reduce the role of chance or of irreversible mixing). But the operations, although they also constitute integrated structures, are essentially reversible: $+n$ is completely canceled out by $-n$. As a consequence, the perceptual structures involve a non-additive composition; indeed, it is this characteristic that the gestaltists use to define the central notion of Gestalt. Now, an operation is rigorously additive, for $2 + 2$ make exactly 4 and not a little more or a little less, as in the realm of perceptual structures. It seems obvious, therefore, that operations, or intelligence in general, do not derive from the perceptual systems. Even if in the preoperatory forms of thought there are intermediate states that resemble the perceptual forms, there is still a fundamental duality of orientation between the irreversibility of perceptual adaptations to specific situations and the reversible constructions peculiar to the logico-mathematical conquests of the operatory intelligence. This duality between irreversible perceptual adaptation and reversible operatory concepts is apparent in the development as well as in the history of scientific thought.

3

THE SEMIOTIC
OR SYMBOLIC FUNCTION

AT THE END of the sensori-motor period, at about one and
a half to two years, there appears a function that is fundamental to the development of later behavior patterns. It
consists in the ability to represent something (a signified
something: object, event, conceptual scheme, etc.) by
means of a "signifier" which is differentiated and which
serves only a representative purpose: language, mental image, symbolic gesture, and so on. Following H. Head and
the specialists in aphasia, we generally refer to this function that gives rise to representation as "symbolic." However, since linguists distinguish between "symbols" and
"signs," we would do better to adopt their term "semiotic
function" to designate those activities having to do with
the differentiated signifiers as a whole.

C

I. *The Semiotic Function and Imitation*

The sensori-motor mechanisms are prerepresentational, and behavior based on the evocation of an absent object is not observed until during the second year. When the scheme of the permanent object is in process of being formed, from about nine to twelve months, there is certainly a search for an object that has disappeared; but since it has just been perceived, the search is part of an action already under way, and a series of clues remains to aid the child to find the object again.

Although representation does not yet exist, the baby forms and uses significations, since every sensori-motor assimilation (including perceptual assimilations) already implies the attribution of a signification, of a meaning. Significations and consequently also a duality between "signified" (the schemes themselves with their content; that is, the action) and "signifiers" are already present. However, these "signifiers" remain perceptual and are not yet differentiated from the "signified." This makes it impossible to talk about semiotic function at this level. An undifferentiated signifier is, in fact, as yet neither a "symbol" nor a "sign" (in the sense of verbal signs). It is by definition an "indicator" (including the "signals" occurring in conditioning, like the sound of the bell that announces food). An indicator is actually undifferentiated from its signified in that it constitutes an aspect of it (whiteness for milk), a part (the visible section for a semi-hidden object), a temporal antecedent (the door that opens for the arrival of Mama), a causal result (a stain), etc.

1. *The Appearance of the Semiotic Function*

In the course of the second year (and continuing from Stage 6 of infancy), however, certain behavior patterns appear which imply the representative evocation of an object or event not present and which consequently presuppose the formation or use of differentiated signifiers, since they must be able to refer to elements not perceptible at the time as well as to those which are present. One can distinguish at least five of these behavior patterns whose appearance is almost simultaneous and which we shall list in order of increasing complexity:

1. First there is *deferred imitation,* that is, imitation which starts after the disappearance of the model. In a behavior pattern of sensori-motor imitation the child begins by imitating in the presence of the model (for example, a movement of the hand), after which he may continue in the absence of the model, though this does not imply any representation in thought. But in the case of a little girl of sixteen months who sees a playmate become angry, scream, and stamp her foot (new sights for her) and who, an hour or two after the playmate's departure, imitates the scene, laughing, the deferred imitation constitutes the beginning of representation, and the imitative gesture the beginning of a differentiated signifier.

2. Then there is *symbolic play* or the game of pretending, which is unknown at the sensori-motor level. The same little girl invented her first symbolic game by pretending to sleep—sitting down and smiling broadly, but closing her eyes, her head to one side, her thumb in her mouth,

and holding a corner of the tablecloth, pretending that it was the corner of her pillow, according to the ritual she observes when she goes to sleep. Shortly afterward she put her stuffed bear to sleep and slid a shell along a box while saying "meow" (she had just seen a cat on a wall). In all these cases the representation is clear-cut and the deferred signifier is an imitative gesture, though accompanied by objects which are becoming symbolic.

3. The *drawing* or graphic image is at first an intermediate stage between play and mental image. It rarely appears before two or two and a half.

4. Then, sooner or later, comes the *mental image,* no trace of which is observed on the sensori-motor level (otherwise discovery of the permanent object would be greatly facilitated). It appears as an internalized imitation.

5. Finally, nascent language permits *verbal evocation* of events that are not occurring at the time. When the little girl says "meow" after the cat has disappeared, verbal representation is added to imitation. When, some time afterward, she says "Anpa bye-bye" (Grandpa went away), pointing to the sloping path he took when he left, the representation is supported either by the differentiated signifier, consisting of the signs of the nascent language, or by both language and mental image.

2. *The Role of Imitation*

Given these first manifestations of the semiotic function, the problem is to understand the mechanism of its formation. This is greatly simplified by the fact that the first four of these five forms of behavior are based on imitation. Moreover, language itself, which, contrary to the preceding behavior patterns, is not invented by the child, is necessarily acquired in a context of imitation. (If it were learned solely by means of a series of conditionings, as is often maintained, it would appear as early as the second month.) Imitation constitutes both the sensori-motor pre-figuration of representation and the transitional phase between the sensori-motor level and the level of behavior that may properly be called representative.

Imitation is first of all a prefiguration of representation. That is to say, it constitutes during the sensori-motor period a kind of representation in physical acts but not yet in thought.[1]

[1] Imitation makes its appearance (with Stages 2 and 3 of infancy) through a kind of contagion or echopraxis. When someone performs in front of the child a gesture the child has just made, the child will repeat the gesture. A little later, the child will imitate any gesture made by an adult, provided that at some time or other this gesture has been performed by the child himself. There is thus at first an assimilation of what the child sees to his own schemes, and a triggering of these schemes. Then a little later the subject attempts to reproduce these models for the sake of the reproduction itself and no longer by automatic assimilation. This marks the appearance of the "prerepresentative" function fulfilled by imitation. Then the child advances rather quickly to the point where he copies gestures that are new to him, but only if they can be performed by visible parts of his own body. An important new phase begins with the imitation of facial movements (opening and closing the mouth or eyes, etc.). The difficulty is then that the child's own face is known to him only by touch and the face of the other person by sight, except for a few rare tactile explorations of the other person's face. Such explorations are very interesting to note at this level, when the child is forming correspondences between the visual and tactilo-kinesthetic sensations in order to extend imitation to the non-visible parts of his body. Until these correspondences are elaborated, imitation of facial movements remains impossible or is accidental. For example, yawning, so contagious later, is not imitated until about the age of one, if it is silent. Once

At the end of the sensori-motor period the child has acquired sufficient virtuosity in the mastery of the imitation thus generalized for deferred imitation to become possible. In fact, representation in action is then liberated from the sensori-motor requirements of direct perceptual copy and reaches an intermediary level where the action, detached from its context, becomes a differentiated signifier and consequently already constitutes in part a representation in thought. With symbolic play and drawing, this transition from representation in action to representation in thought is reinforced. The "pretending to sleep" of the example cited above is still only an action detached from its context, but it is also a symbol capable of generalization. With the mental image, which follows, imitation is no longer merely deferred but internalized, and the representation that it makes possible, thus dissociated from any external action in favor of the internal sketches or outlines of actions which will henceforth support it, is now ready to become thought. The acquisition of language, rendered accessible in these contexts of imitation, finally overlays the whole process, providing a contact with other people which is far more effective than imitation alone, and thus permitting the nascent representation to increase its powers with the aid of communication.

---

the correspondences have been established by means of a series of indications (auditory, etc.), imitation is generalized and plays an important role in the child's knowledge of his own body in analogy with the bodies of others. It is no exaggeration, therefore, to regard imitation as a kind of representation in action. Baldwin goes one step further, seeing it as an essential instrument in the complementary formation of the other and the self.

3. *Symbols and Signs*

Broadly speaking, the semiotic function gives rise to two kinds of instruments: *symbols,* which are "motivated" —that is, although they are differentiated signifiers, they do present some resemblance to the things signified; and *signs,* which are arbitrary or conventional. Symbols, being motivated, may be created by the individual by himself. The first symbols of the child's play are good examples of these individual creations, which obviously do not exclude later collective symbolisms. Deferred imitation, symbolic play, and the graphic or mental image thus depend directly on imitation, not as transmissions of ready-made external models (for there is an imitation of oneself as well as of others, as is shown by the example of the game of simulating sleep), but rather as transitions from prerepresentation in action to internal representation, or thought. Signs, on the other hand, being conventional, are necessarily collective. The child receives them, therefore, through the medium of imitation, but this time as an acquisition of external models. However, he immediately fashions them to suit himself and uses them, as we shall see later (pages 84 ff.).

II. *Symbolic Play*

Symbolic play is the apogee of children's play. Even more than the two or three other forms of play which we shall discuss, it corresponds to the essential function that play fulfills in the life of the child. Obliged to adapt himself constantly to a social world of elders whose interests and rules remain external to him, and to a physical world which he understands only slightly, the child does not succeed as we adults do in satisfying the affective and even intellectual needs of his personality through these adaptations. It is indispensable to his affective and intellectual equilibrium, therefore, that he have available to him an area of activity whose motivation is not adaptation to reality but, on the contrary, assimilation of reality to the self, without coercions or sanctions. Such an area is play, which transforms reality by assimilation to the needs of the self, whereas imitation (when it constitutes an end in itself) is accommodation to external models. Intelligence constitutes an equilibration between assimilation and accommodation.[2]

Furthermore, the essential instrument of social adaptation is language, which is not invented by the child but transmitted to him in ready-made, compulsory, and collective forms. These are not suited to expressing the child's needs or his living experience of himself. The child, therefore, needs a means of self-expression, that is, a system of signifiers constructed by him and capable of being bent to his wishes. Such is the system of symbols characteristic of symbolic play. These symbols are borrowed from imitation as instruments, but not used to accurately picture external reality. Rather, imitation serves as a means of evocation to achieve playful assimilation. Thus, symbolic play is not merely an assimilation of reality to the self, as is play in general, but an assimilation made possible (and reinforced)

[2] Jean Piaget, *Play, Dreams and Imitation in Childhood* (New York: W. W. Norton, 1951; London: Routledge and Kegan Paul, 1951).

by a symbolic "language" that is developed by the self and is capable of being modified according to its needs.[3]

The function of assimilation fulfilled by symbolic play is manifested in a great variety of forms, most of them primarily affective, but sometimes serving cognitive interests. A little girl who while on vacation had asked various questions about the mechanics of the bells observed on an old village church steeple, now stood stiff as a ramrod beside her father's desk, making a deafening noise. "You're bothering me, you know. Can't you see I'm working?" "Don't talk to me," replied the little girl. "I'm a church." Similarly, the child was deeply impressed by a plucked duck she'd seen on the kitchen table, and that evening

[3] There exist three principal categories of play, and a fourth which serves as a transition between symbolic play and non-playful activities or "serious" adaptations. (1) *Exercise play,* a primitive form of play, and the only kind that occurs at the sensori-motor level and is retained in part. It does not involve symbolism or any specific play technique, but consists in repeating, for the pleasure of it, activities acquired elsewhere in the course of adaptation. For example, the child, having discovered by chance the possibility of swinging a suspended object, at first repeats the action in order to adapt to it and understand it, which is not play. Then, having done this, he uses this behavior pattern for simple "functional pleasure" (K. Bühler) or for the pleasure of causing an effect and of confirming his newly acquired skill (something the adult does too, say, with a new car or a new television set). (2) *Symbolic play,* whose characteristics we have seen, reaches its apogee between two to three and five to six. (3) *Games with rules* (marbles, hopscotch, etc.), which are transmitted socially from child to child and thus increase in importance with the enlargement of the child's social life. (4) Finally, out of symbolic play there develop *games of construction,* which are initially imbued with play symbolism but tend later to constitute genuine adaptations (mechanical constructions, etc.) or solutions to problems and intelligent creations.

C*

was found lying on a sofa, so still that she was thought to be sick. At first she did not answer questions; then in a faraway voice she said, "I'm the dead duck!" The symbolism of play, then, may even fulfill the function of what for an adult would be internal language. Rather than simply recalling an interesting or impressive event, the child has need of a more direct symbolism which enables him to relive the event.[4]

These multiple functions of symbolic play have inspired several theories that attempt to explain all forms of play. They are today quite out of date. (An extreme example is G. S. Hall's hypothesis of hereditary recapitulation, which in the realm of play anticipated Jung's most adventurous ideas on unconscious symbols.) The most important of these early theories is that of Karl Groos, who was the first to discover that the play of children (and of animals) has an essential functional value and is not simply a diversion. He saw play as preliminary training for the future activities of the individual—which is true but

---

[4] It is, primarily, affective conflicts that reappear in symbolic play, however. If there is a scene at lunch, for example, one can be sure that an hour or two afterward it will be re-created with dolls and will be brought to a happier solution. Either the child disciplines her doll more intelligently than her parents did her, or in play she accepts what she had not accepted at lunch (such as finishing a bowl of soup she does not like, especially if here it is the doll who finishes it symbolically). Similarly, if the child has been frightened by a big dog, in a symbolic game things will be arranged so that dogs will no longer be mean or else children will become brave. Generally speaking, symbolic play helps in the resolution of conflicts and also in the compensation of unsatisfied needs, the inversion of roles (such as obedience and authority), the liberation and extension of the self, etc.

obvious if you say that play, like every general function, is useful to the individual's development, but which becomes meaningless if you go into details. Is the child who plays that he is a church preparing to become a church warden, and the child who plays that he is a dead duck preparing to become an ornithologist? A much more profound theory is that of F. J. J. Buytendijk, who relates play to the laws of "infantile dynamics." However, these laws are not in themselves laws of play and in order to account for the specific nature of play it seems necessary, as we proposed above, to refer to a pole of assimilation to the self as distinct from both the accommodative pole of imitation and the equilibrium between the two (intelligence).[5] In symbolic play this systematic assimilation takes the form of a particular use of the semiotic function—namely, the creation of symbols at will in order to express everything in the child's life experience that cannot be formulated and assimilated by means of language alone.

This symbolism centering on the self [6] is not limited to formulating and nourishing the child's conscious interests.

[5] In a penetrating and lively work, *Jeux de l'esprit* (Paris: Editions du Scarabée, 1963), J. O. Grandjouan finds fault with the interpretation of play in terms of the primacy of assimilation. He puts the emphasis on games with rules, whereas the play characteristic of early childhood, it seems to us, is symbolic play, which is related by all the intermediate stages to non-playful thought and which differs from it, therefore, only in the degree of assimilation of reality to the self.

[6] We no longer call it "egocentric," as one of us once did, in deference to the criticisms from many psychologists who are still not familiar with the practice in the exact sciences of using a term only in accordance with the definitions proposed, irrespective of its popular meanings and associations.

Symbolic play frequently deals with unconscious conflicts: sexual interests, defense against anxiety, phobias, aggression or identification with aggressors, withdrawal from fear of risk or competition, etc. Here the symbolism of play resembles the symbolism of the dream, to such a degree that child psychoanalysis makes frequent use of play materials (Melanie Klein, Anna Freud, and others). However Freudian theory has long interpreted the symbolism of the dream (not to mention the perhaps inevitable exaggerations involved in the interpretation of symbols when one does not possess sufficient means of checking results) as a disguisement based on mechanisms of repression and censorship. The vague boundaries between the conscious and the unconscious as evidenced by the child's symbolic play suggest rather that the symbolism of the dream is analogous to the symbolism of play, because the sleeper loses at the same time the rational use of language, the sense of reality, and the deductive or logical instruments of his intelligence. Involuntarily, therefore, he finds himself in the situation of symbolic assimilation which the child seeks for its own sake. Jung saw that this oneiric symbolism consists of a kind of primitive language, which corresponds to what we have just seen of symbolic play, and he concentrated on certain symbols and showed their universal nature. But, without any proof (lack of concern for verification is even more noticeable in the Jungian school than it is in the Freudian schools), he argued from the universality of these symbols that they are innate and went on from there to the theory of hereditary archetypes. Yet one would no doubt find the same universality in the laws of the child's play symbolism; and since the child is anterior to the man and was so even in prehistoric times, it may be in the ontogenetic approach to the formative mechanisms of the semiotic function that the solution to the problem will be found.

III. *Drawing*

Drawing is a form of the semiotic function which should be considered as being halfway between symbolic play and the mental image. It is like symbolic play in its functional pleasure and autotelism, and like the mental image in its effort at imitating the real. G. H. Luquet classifies drawing as a game. Yet, even in its initial forms, there is no question of a free assimilation of reality to the subject's own schemes. Like the mental image, it is closer to imitative accommodation. In fact, it constitutes sometimes a preparation for, sometimes a product of imitative accommodation. Between the graphic image and the internal image (Luquet's "internal model") there exist innumerable interactions, since both phenomena derive directly from imitation.[7]

In his celebrated studies on children's drawings, Luquet [8] proposed stages and interpretations which are still

---

[7] Actually, the very first form of drawing does not seem imitative and has characteristics of pure play, but it is a play of exercise: this is the scribbling the child of two to two and a half engages in when he is given a pencil. Very soon, however, the subject thinks he recognizes forms in his aimless scribble, with the result that soon thereafter he tries to render a model from memory, however poor a likeness his graphic expression may be from an objective point of view. As soon as this intention exists, drawing becomes imitation and image.

[8] G. H. Luquet, *Le Dessin enfantin* (Paris: Alcan, 1927).

valid today. Before him, two contrary opinions were maintained. One group held that the first drawings of children
are essentially realistic, since they keep to actual models,
and that drawings of the imagination do not appear until
rather late. The other group insisted that idealization was
evidenced in early drawings. Luquet seems to have settled
the dispute conclusively by showing that until about eight
or nine a child's drawing is essentially realistic in intention,
though the subject begins by drawing what he *knows*
about a person or an object long before he can draw what
he actually *sees*. This observation is a fundamental one
whose full significance will become apparent when we
consider the mental image, because it too is a conceptualization before it culminates in good perceptive copies.

The realism of drawing thus passes through different
phases. Luquet uses the phrase "fortuitous realism" to refer to the realism of the scribble whose meaning is discovered in the act of making it. Then comes "failed realism,"
or the phase of synthetic incapacity, in which the elements
of the copy are juxtaposed instead of being coordinated
into a whole: a hat well above the head or buttons along-
side the body. The little man, one of the commonest first
drawings, passes through an extremely interesting stage:
that of the "tadpole man," which consists of a head provided with threadlike appendages (the legs), or with arms
and legs, but without a trunk.

Then comes the period of "intellectual realism," where
the drawing has already evolved beyond the primitive
scribblings, but where it pictures the conceptual attributes
of the model, without concern for visual perspective. For
example, a face seen in profile will have a second eye because a man has two eyes, or a horseman, in addition to

his visible leg, will have a leg which can be seen through the horse. Similarly, one will see potatoes in the ground, if that is where they are, or in a man's stomach.[9]

At about eight or nine, "intellectual realism" is succeeded by "visual realism," which presents two new features. First, the drawing now represents only what is visible from one particular perspective. A profile now has only one eye, etc., as would be seen from the side, and the concealed parts of objects are no longer visibly represented. (Thus, one sees only the top of a tree behind a house, and no longer the whole tree.) Also, objects in the background are made gradually smaller (receding lines) in relation to objects in the foreground. Second, the objects in the drawing are arranged according to an overall plan (axes of coordinates) and to their geometrical proportions.

The value of Luquet's stages is twofold. They constitute a remarkable introduction to the study of the mental image, which, as we shall see, obeys laws that are closer to those of conceptualization than to those of perception.

[9] In addition to this "transparency," one observes that children draw configurations as if seen from different angles and as if a three-dimensional object were flattened out (pseudo-rabatment). Luquet mentions a drawing of a cart in which the horse is seen from the side, the inside of the cart is seen from above, and the wheels are flattened out into a horizontal plane. A similar procedure is used to represent a narrative. Whereas adult imagery conventionally presents only one segment of many simultaneous events per drawing, without introducing, within the same drawing, actions that are chronologically successive, the child, like some primitive painters, uses one drawing to present a chain of chronological events. Thus one will see a mountain with five or six figures on it, each of which represents the same person in successive positions.

Moreover, they attest to a remarkable convergence with the evolution of the spontaneous geometry of the child.[10]

The first spatial intuitions of the child are, in fact, topological rather than projective or consistent with Euclidean metric geometry.[11] Up to the age of four, for example, squares, rectangles, circles, ellipses, etc., are all represented by a closed curve without straight lines or angles. Topologically, squares and circles are the same figure. Crosses, arcs, etc., are all represented by an open curve. At this same age, however, children can produce quite accurate copies of a closed figure with a little circle inside. The topological relation of the inside circle to the enclosing one, or even the relation between a closed figure and a

[10] Jean Piaget and Bärbel Inhelder, *The Child's Conception of Space* (London: Routledge and Kegan Paul, 1956).

[11] *Editor's Note*: For the sake of the reader who may not be familiar with mathematics, let us briefly describe topology, projective geometry, and Euclidean geometry. Topology, sometimes nicknamed "rubber-sheet geometry," is concerned with the relationships between points, lines, and regions that are not disturbed when the space is stretched or compressed or distorted. If two regions drawn on a sheet of rubber have a common boundary, that fact remains true no matter how the rubber sheet is stretched. The straightness of a line or the shape of a region is changed if the sheet is stretched; therefore these are not topological properties.

Projective properties of a figure are those that are not changed if the figure is projected onto any plane surface as when it casts a shadow. The shadow of a straight line is always straight, but its shadow may be shorter or longer depending upon the slant of the surface on which its shadow is projected. The shadow of a circle is not circular, but it is always some form of ellipse.

Euclidean properties are those actual lengths and measurements of a figure constant, as when a figure is merely translated or copied in another spot.

circle on its boundary is represented by children who are quite incapable of copying a square correctly.

Although the "intellectual realism" of the child's drawing shows no awareness of perspective or metrical relationships, it does show topological relationships: proximity, separation, enclosure, closedness, and so on. And these topological intuitions are followed, after the age of seven or eight, by both projective intuitions and a sense of Euclidean metric geometry. At this age there appear the two essential elements of "visual realism" in drawing. Moreover, at this age the child discovers the end-on sighting methods for guaranteeing the projective straight line and also understands elementary perspective. The child becomes capable of drawing an object not as he sees it but as it would be seen by an observer located to the right of or opposite the child. At nine to ten the child is able to choose correctly from among several drawings all representing three mountains or three buildings as they would appear from specified viewing points. At this time too the child becomes aware of the vectorial straight line (conservation of direction), the group structure representing displacements, and measurement (of objects by means of a standard unit as discussed in Chapter 4). He can also realize that similar figures may not be identical in size but they must be proportional. Finally he can understand measurement in two and three dimensions by means of a system of coordinates. From the age of nine or ten (but, interestingly, seldom before that) the average child becomes capable of anticipating that the water surface in a jar will be horizontal even if the jar is tilted at various angles, and that the line of the mast of a boat floating on this water will stay vertical. (The experimenter draws the outlines of the jars and the child indicates the horizontal and vertical lines by way of references external to the figure.[12])

IV. *Mental Images* [13]

Associationist psychology regards the image as an extension of perception and thinking as consisting of the association between sensations and mental images. We have seen (Chapter 1) that in fact "associations" are always assimilations. There are at least two good reasons to doubt the derivation of mental images from perception. Neurologically, an imagined bodily movement is accompanied by the same pattern of electrical waves, whether cortical (EEG) or muscular (EMG), as the physical execution of the movement. That is, the imagining of a movement involves a kind of sketch of that movement. The second objection is genetic; if the image were merely a prolongation of a perception, it would appear from birth. Yet no evidence of it is observed during the sensori-motor period. It

[12] Thus we see that the evolution of drawing is inseparable from the whole structuration of space, according to the different stages of this development. It is not surprising, then, that the child's drawing serves as a test of his intellectual development. In this connection, F. Goodenough, A. Rey, and others have made useful studies, with standardized scales that concentrate particularly on development as seen in the "draw-a-man test." Drawing has also been used as an affective index, notably by the psychoanalyst S. Morgenstern in the case of children afflicted with selective autism.

[13] Jean Piaget and Bärbel Inhelder, *L'Image mentale chez l'enfant* (Paris: Presses Universitaires de France, 1966).

seems to begin only at the time of the appearance of the semiotic function.[14]

1. *The Problems Raised by the Image*

It would seem, therefore, that mental images are relatively late in appearing because they are the result of an internalized imitation. Their resemblance to perception does not attest to a direct derivation from perception but is, rather, due to the fact that the imitation involved in imagery actively copies the perceptual data, and may even elicit sensations in the same way as an imagined movement elicits muscular contractions.

As for the relationship between images and thought, Binet and the German psychologists of the Wurzburg school (from K. Marbe and O. Külpe to K. Bühler) have shown the existence of what they call imageless thought. One can imagine an object, but the judgment that affirms or denies its existence is not itself characterized by an

[14] Psychoanalysts assume a very precocious capacity to hallucinate the realization of desires, but they have yet to furnish proof of this. Recently there have been indications that such verification would be possible, for N. Kleitman and E. Aserinsky have succeeded in taking electroretinograms during sleep which seem to correspond to visual images of dreaming (rapid eye movements distinct from the habitual slow movements). W. Dement has applied this technique to newborn babies, but he finds a much greater incidence of rapid eye movements than at later stages in the individual's development. A greater incidence of these movements has been observed in the opossum (a living fossil) than in the cat or in man. This seems to indicate that rapid eye movements have other functions (cleansing or detoxication) and do not necessarily involve actual visual imagery. Dement concludes, therefore, that his and E. A. Wolpert's studies do not confirm the psychoanalytic interpretation of the dream.

image. This finding implies that judgments and operations are not images, but it does not rule out the possibility that the image can play a role in thinking as a complementary symbolic auxiliary to language. Language itself never represents anything but concepts or concrete objects seen as classes with only one member (for example, "my father"). The adult, as does the child, needs a system of signifiers dealing not with concepts but with objects as such and with the whole past perceptual experience of the subject. This role has been assigned to the image, and its quality of "symbol" (as opposed to "sign") permits it to acquire a more or less adequate, although schematized, resemblance to the objects symbolized.

The problem, then, throughout the child's development, is to describe the relationship between imaginal symbolism and the preoperatory or operatory mechanisms of thought.[15]

2. *Two Types of Images*

The studies we have conducted for several years on the development of mental images in the child between four or five and ten or twelve indicate a clear-cut difference between images characteristic of the preoperatory level (be-

[15] This problem is parallel to the problem of the relationship between perception and intelligence (Chapter 2, pages 43 ff.), for perception, imitation, and the image correspond to the figurative aspects of the cognitive functions, as opposed to the operative aspects (actions and operations). In both cases, the need is first of all to determine whether the figurative element (image and perception alike) prefigures certain operatory structures (concepts, etc.), and in what sense, filiation or analogous formation. Next we must determine whether the evolution of the figurative elements (images and perceptions) follows an independent course in the form of a simple internal development, or whether it depends upon the help of externals such as operatory factors.

fore seven or eight) and those of the operatory levels, which at this stage appear to be strongly influenced by the operations.

First of all, it is necessary to distinguish two broad categories of mental images: *reproductive images*, which are limited to evoking sights that have been perceived previously, and *anticipatory images*, which envisage movements or transformations as well as their results, although the subject has not previously observed them (as one can envisage how a geometric figure would look if it were transformed). Reproductive images may include static configurations, movements (changes of position), and transformations (changes of form), for these three kinds of realities occur constantly in the perceptual experience of the subject. If the image proceeded from perception alone, one would then find at every age these three classes of reproductive image (static, kinetic, and transformational) in frequencies corresponding to those actually occurring in the child's environment.

Our studies indicate, however, that the mental images of the child at the preoperatory level are almost exclusively static. He has systematic difficulties in reproducing in imagery movements or transformations he has observed. It is not until the level of concrete operations (after seven to eight) that children are capable of reproducing movements and transformations, and by this stage the child can also anticipate in his imagery movements and transformations. This seems to prove (1) that imaginal reproduction even of well-known movements or transformations involves either anticipation or a reanticipation, and (2) that both reproductive and anticipatory images of movements or transformations depend on the operations that make it possible for the child to understand these processes. The formation of mental images cannot precede understanding.

3. Copy Images

To introduce some clarity into this complex situation, let us begin by examining what we may call "copy images," in which the model remains in view of the subject or has just been perceived the instant before. There is here no deferred evocation after several days or weeks, as there is in tests relating to the translations or rotations of models present in the child's experience but not shown when he is questioned.[16]

In an experiment made with B. Matalon, for example, a horizontal rod 20 centimeters long was placed on a sheet of paper and the child was asked three times to draw it immediately to its right without leaving any intervening space: (1) after imagining that it describes an arc of 180° to arrive at this position, (2) after imagining that it is simply pushed (translation) into this same position, and (3) as a simple graphic copy without allusion to any movement, and still in the same position. (Naturally, the order is varied: 1, 2, 3; 3, 2, 1; etc.)

The first thing we observe is in fact a widespread phenomenon: at the age of five the graphic copy (3) is shorter than the model by about −13.5 percent (a 20-centimeter rod is drawn 17.3 centimeters long on the average). This systematic shortening diminishes with age (−10.5 percent at seven, etc.) and disappears in the adult. This phenomenon is also observed when young subjects are asked

[16] The copy image consists of a simple physical imitation (graphic or gestural), as opposed to the mental image, which is an internalized imitation.

to draw with their fingers on the desk without a pencil, but it is not present when the child is asked to show the length in the air by means of two raised index fingers. A shortening of this kind, which is found in all the other experiments, seems to have only one explanation. Accustomed to judging lengths in an ordinal rather than in a metrical fashion, that is, by the order of the points of arrival rather than by the interval between the extremities (except in the case of the raised index fingers), the young subjects concentrate on not going beyond the terminal boundary of the model. It does not matter if the copy is shorter (for in this case it is still within the length of the model); the essential thing is that it not be too long.

In the case of conditions (1) and (2), the drawings produced are even shorter (−20.5 percent for rotation and −19 percent for translation at the age of five). In these cases, graphic imitations of the length of the model are even shorter, although the model remains in the child's sight and the copy is made in the same place as in (3). Thus we see the complexity of even a simple pencil stroke. The intention to imitate the length of the model requires a plan of execution whose laws are closer to conceptualization than they are to simple perception.[17]

[17] To turn to gestural copies, relating this time to kinetic models (for the kinetic copy image is naturally easier than the deferred evocation of a movement by means of mental images as such)—together with A. Etienne, we asked children from three to six to reproduce different, very easy models. Two checkers were set in motion in such a way as to describe movements of launching or pulling (cf. Michotte's experiments mentioned in Chapter 2, pages 33–34), symmetrical backward and forward movement, crossing, etc., and the subjects were requested to reproduce these movements, also with checkers, either while the movements were

4. *Kinetic and Transformational Images*

Turning to mental images proper, let us remember first how difficult it is to measure them experimentally, since they are internal. We have to resort to indirect methods, within which cross-checking affords some degree of certainty: the child's drawing, the child's choices from among drawings prepared in advance, gestural indications, and his verbal comments (hazardous, but possible if used along with the other three techniques). From this point of view, the simplest of the kinetic reproductive images seems to us, as to F. Frank and T. Bang, to be one square placed on top of another (the upper side of the second being adjacent to the lower side of the first). The problem is to anticipate a slight movement on the part of the top square. One has first made sure that the child knows how to draw a fairly exact copy of the model; that is, of one square partially superimposed on another and partially projecting beyond the edge. After five and a half, the child can do this; yet, on the average, he is unable to make an anticipatory drawing of the same situation until he is seven or older. The young subjects confine themselves to drawing the square in its initial position, or beside the other square. When they succeed in drawing a slight change of position,

---

being slowly executed or immediately afterward. We observed numerous errors in the copies because of the predominance of "good forms" (symmetrical movements) over random forms. In addition, and more important, until the age of five a gap was observed (very obvious at three and diminishing afterward) between simultaneous reproductions and reproductions done immediately afterward. Those do not become as accurate as simultaneous reproductions until the age of six. This is a first and very significant indication of the difficulty of kinetic images.

they shorten the top (mobile) square or lengthen the bottom one so that the mobile square does not go beyond the boundary of the stationary one! [18]

Equally surprising in view of the frequency of the everyday models, which might have assured an accurate representation, are the reproductive images made of a 90-degree rotation of a rod (like the movements of the hand of a watch or an upright stick that falls to the ground) or of the "somersault" of a tube that describes a rotation of 180 degrees. In the first, the rod is nailed at its base so that it moves steadily around a fixed pivotal point. But the young subjects pay no attention to this fact, although it is

[18] When the squares are presented so that one entirely covers the other (an experiment made with F. Frank and J. Bliss, using transparent squares, one with red edges and the other with black edges), the child, when invited to anticipate a gradual change of position, has no difficulty drawing the projecting of the red-edged square beyond the black-edged square, but he refuses to draw the parallel side of the red-edged square which can be seen through the middle of the black-edged one. This reaction is all the more curious since in his spontaneous drawings the child often indicates "transparencies," to use Luquet's expression. Such "transparencies" are illegitimate, however, as when the invisible leg of a horseman is "seen" through a horse drawn from the side. When the squares are actually transparent, the refusal to draw the red side which divides the black-edged square is related to a problem of boundary, this time with reference to an intersection. The child has the impression that by dividing the black-edged square in two through the introduction of a red line belonging to the other square, he would alter the image of the black-edged square, whose surface must remain intact. As in the case of the refusal to go beyond the boundary, we have here a kind of "pseudo-conservation" peculiar to the image which is all the more curious in that it is respected at the expense of the conservation of the surface (one square above the other) or the conservation of one side (one square covering the other overlapping squares).

clearly pointed out to them, and draw trajectories forming right angles (as if the rod traveled the length of its initial and final positions or the length of their opposites in the form of a square) or intersecting at any angle no matter which. In the case of the tube, it is colored red and blue at the ends and projects beyond the edge of a box, responding to a pressure of the finger on the free end which causes it to turn upside down and fall in an inverted position a few centimeters from the box. Subjects who anticipate rather well the transposition of the colored ends (about 50 percent at five and 100 percent at eight) do not manage until a later age to draw two or three of the intermediary positions of the tube (42 percent succeed at seven and 60 percent at eight) and, remarkably enough, are not much more successful in imitating the movement of inversion by a slow-motion gesture while holding the tube in their hands (45 percent at seven and 70 percent at eight, as shown in studies made with E. Schmid-Kitsikis). We see that movements of the most ordinary kind (for what child has not himself turned somersaults?) give rise to rather poor kinetic reproductive images up to and even after the onset of the concrete operations (seven to eight).

As an example of a transformational image, we can cite a detailed study carried out with F. Frank, involving the unbending of an arc (of flexible wire) into a straight line or, conversely, the bending of the straight line into an arc. Here again, children have great difficulty in imagining the intermediary positions. In imagining the outcome of the transformation, young subjects (until about seven) draw figures with a marked boundary effect. They draw the straight line so that its ends correspond to those of the arc:

Thus the straight line resulting from the unbending of the arc is underestimated by −34 percent at five. Similarly, the arc resulting from the curving of the straight line is overestimated by +29 percent at five, so that its ends will meet those of the straight line.

It is no exaggeration, then, to speak of the static quality of preoperatory images. Kinetic and transformational images are possible only after seven or eight, and this as a result of anticipations or reanticipations which are no doubt themselves based on operatory comprehension.

5. *Images and Operations*

Turning now to direct analysis of the relationship between imaginary representation and the operation, we shall consider only two examples, for they all demonstrate similar phenomena. The technique consists in presenting the customary tests for conservation of quantity (see Chapter 4, pages 97 ff.), but instead of questioning the subject about the transformations he has just observed, you ask him to anticipate what is going to happen by imagining the phases and results of the transformations. In the test of the conservation of liquids in which there is a standard glass A, a narrower glass B, and a wider glass C, subjects are asked to anticipate the result of pouring the liquid from A to B and C, and in particular to indicate the levels that will be reached by the water. Two interesting results (obtained by S. Taponier) are observed in the reactions of preoperatory subjects (five to seven). The majority anticipate that the levels in the three glasses will be the same and thus they predict that the quantity of liquid will be unchanged (conservation but for the wrong reason). It is after they actually see the results of the pouring—that is, the water rises higher in *B* than in *A* and less high in *C*—that they begin to deny all conservation of quantity.

However, a second group of subjects, smaller than the first, foresee correctly that the water will rise higher in *B* and less high in *C* than in *A*, but conclude from this in advance that the quantity of liquid is not the same. When you ask these children to pour equal amounts of water in *A* and *B*, they maintain the same level in both glasses. Even if the reproductive image of the levels is accurate, this is not sufficient for a judgment of conservation, as there is a lack of understanding of compensation. The child may say the water will rise higher in *B* "because the glass is narrower," but he does not therefore conclude that "higher × narrower = same quantity." For him, the narrowness of *B* is only an empirical indication that enables him to foresee (but not to understand) the rise in the level of the water.

Another experiment gives parallel results. A child of five or six places twelve red counters opposite twelve blue ones to make sure there is an equal number of each. Yet if you space out either the blue or the red counters, he concludes that the longer row contains more elements. The question arises whether this lack of conservation is due to a difficulty in imagining these displacements and a possible return of the displaced elements to their original positions. We therefore constructed a fan-shaped apparatus designed so that each blue counter in the compressed upper row communicated with a red counter in the spaced-out lower row by means of a lane within which the lower counter could move upward until it met its blue counterpart. This arrangement in no way altered the child's ideas. Even when he imagines the movements perfectly, he neverthe-less concludes, placing himself at a crosswise rather than a lengthwise vantage point, that the number of counters in-creases when the row grows longer and decreases when it grows shorter. After S. Taponier had studied the effects of successive displacements, M. Aboudaram introduced a mechanism whereby the twelve counters of the mobile row could move up or down as a unit. The reactions remained the same.

From these and other facts, one can conclude that men-tal images are merely a system of symbols which provide a more or less accurate but, generally speaking, delayed translation of the subjects' preoperatory or operatory level of comprehension. The image is far from sufficient to give rise to operatory structurations. At the very most, the image, when it is sufficiently adequate (cf. the representa-tion of water levels in the second group of subjects cited above), can serve to refine the subjects' awareness of states which the operation will later connect by means of revers-ible transformations. But the image in itself remains static and discontinuous (cf. the "cinematographic process" which Bergson attributed to the intelligence itself, ignoring the operation, and characterizing only image-representa-tion). After the age of seven or eight, the image becomes anticipatory and so better able to serve as a base for the operations. This progress is not the result of an internal or autonomous modification of the images, however, but rather of the intervention of external factors due to the development of the operations. These have their source in action itself, and not in image-symbolism, or in the system of verbal signs or language that we shall now discuss.

V. *Memory and the Structure of Image-Memories*

Too little research has been done on the memory of the child, and what research there has been has centered primarily on the measuring of performance. For example, by reading fifteen words to the subject and finding out how many he retained after one minute, Claparède observed a gradual increase with age to an average of eight words in the adult.

The most important factor in the development of memory, however, is its gradual organization. There are two types of memory: the memory of *recognition*, which operates only in the presence of an object already encountered and which consists in recognizing it; and the memory of *evocation*, which consists in evoking the object in its absence by means of an image-memory. The memory of recognition is very precocious (it exists in the lower invertebrates) and is necessarily related to action-schemes or habits. In the newborn child, its roots are to be sought in the schemes of elementary sensori-motor assimilation: the baby recognizes the nipple during nursing and distinguishes it from the surrounding skin if it has slipped out of his mouth; the baby recognizes an object which he has been watching if it is lost from sight for an instant; and so on. Evocation memory, mental images, the first beginnings of language (linked together by Janet when he speaks of the appearance of "recounting of events") start more or less simultaneously. This complex of new behavior patterns raises an essential problem: is it independent of or

dependent on the general schematism of actions and operations? [19]

In the light of these remarks, the problem of memory is
primarily a problem of delimitation. Not all conservation
of the past is memory; all schemes (from the sensori-motor
schemes to the operatory schemes of classification, seriation, etc.) continue to function independently of "memory"; in other words, the memory of a scheme is the scheme
itself. What is commonly called memory, then, once rid of
the remnants of facultative psychology, is simply the figurative aspect of the systems of schemes as a whole, from
the elementary sensori-motor schemes in which the figurative aspect is perceptual recognition to the highest schemes
whose figurative and mnemonic aspect is the image-
memory.

[19] Bergson sought to introduce a radical opposition between
the image-memory and the motor-memory of the "*mémoire habi-
tude*" (habit-memory) (which is also related to recognition, for
every habit presupposes the recognition of indications). But this is
the introspection of a philosopher, for if one studies the image-
memory in its development one sees that it is also inseparable from
action. For example, with F. Frank and J. Bliss we studied the
memory, after several days, of an arrangement of cubes, tested
under three different conditions: (1) the child had merely looked
at them; (2) he had actively copied the arrangement; and (3) he
had watched an adult arrange the cubes. (The sequence of the
conditions was varied.) Actively copying the arrangement gives
better results than perception, and learning in the order action-
perception succeeds better than in the order perception-action
(with an interval of at least a week). The perception of adult activity adds almost nothing to the perception of the result alone. The
memory-image is therefore itself related to schemes of action, and
one finds at least ten intermediate stages between motor-memory
with simple recognition and pure evocation in images independent
of action.

On this basis we have undertaken a series of studies which are far from complete but whose results are nevertheless instructive. For example, working with H. Sinclair, we presented ten sticks seriated according to their differences in length, and after a week asked the child to reproduce them by gesture or drawing. We worked with two groups of subjects: the first simply looked at the sticks, and the second described them verbally. Finally, we determined the operatory level of the subject with respect to seriation. The most important result obtained is that, with significant regularity, subjects produce a drawing that corresponds to their operatory level (pairs, uncoordinated short series, or ııı ||| ||| , etc.) rather than to the configuration presented. In other words, memory causes the schemes corresponding to the child's level to predominate: the image-memory relates to this scheme rather than to the perceptual model.[20]

[20] Another study (with J. Bliss) concerned the transitive nature of equalities. A long, narrow glass *A* contains the same quantity as an ordinary glass *B*, and *B* contains the same quantity as a short, wide glass *C*. These equalities are confirmed by transfer of the contents of *A* to *B'* (the equivalent of *B*) and back to *A* and from *C* to *B''* (the equivalent of *B* and *B'*) and back to *C*. Subjects are tested to determine what is retained of these events after an hour and after a week. Here too the child retains what he has understood rather than what he has seen. This is not so obvious as one might think. Subjects at an elementary stage, in particular, draw the transfer from *B* to *C* and vice versa as if the two movements were simultaneous. "But didn't one happen before the other?" "No, both at the same time." "But then the liquids get all mixed up?" *A* goes into *B'* at the same time as it returns, etc.; the process has no transitive relation. The fact that the child has not understood and cannot memorize relationships that he has not understood goes without saying. Yet he might have retained the successive quality of the events perceived. On the contrary, however; he

Six months later, the same subjects provided a second drawing from memory (they had not seen the model again). This consisted in a series which, in 80 percent of the cases, was slightly superior to the first (threes instead of twos, little series instead of threes, etc.). Intellectual progress in the scheme resulted in progress in memory.

As for the conservation of memories themselves, according to some authorities (Freud, Bergson), memories accumulate in the unconscious, where they are forgotten or remain ready to be evoked. According to others (Pierre Janet), remembering is a reconstruction comparable to that carried out by the historian (through testimony, inferences, etc.). W. G. Penfield's recent experiments on the reactivation of memories by electrical stimulation of the temporal lobes suggest a certain degree of conservation, but numerous observations (and the existence of false but vivid memories) also show that reconstruction plays a part. The connection between memories and schemes of action suggested by the preceding facts, along with the schematization of memories as such studied by F. Bartlett,[21] makes such a reconciliation conceivable by emphasizing the importance of motor or operatory elements at all levels of memory. Since, moreover, the image which occurs in image-memory constitutes an internalized imitation, which also includes a motor element, the conservation of particular memories can easily be reconciled with such a context of possible interpretation.

---

schematizes them in terms of intellectual rather than experienced schemes! The following stages are also in strict correlation with the operatory level of the subjects.

[21] F. C. Bartlett, *Remembering* (Cambridge: Cambridge University Press, 1932).

D

VI. *Language*

In the normal child, language appears at about the same time as the other forms of semiotic thought. In the deaf-mute, on the other hand, articulate language does not appear until well after deferred imitation, symbolic play, and the mental image. This seems to indicate that language is derived genetically, since its social or educational transmission presupposes the preliminary development of these individual forms of *semiosis*. However, this development, as is proved by the case of deaf-mutes, can occur independent of language.[22] Furthermore, deaf-mutes, in their collective life, manage to elaborate a gestural language which is of keen interest. It is both social and based on imitative signifiers that occur in an individual form in deferred imitation, in symbolic play, and the image, which is relatively close to symbolic play. Because of its adaptive properties rather than its playful purpose, this gestural language, if it were universal, would constitute an independent and original form of semiotic function. In normal individuals it is rendered unnecessary by the transmission of the collective system of verbal signs associated with articulate language.

[22] One finds in the chimpanzee a beginning of symbolic function which enables him, for example, to save tokens with which to obtain fruits from an automatic dispenser (experiment by J. B. Wolfe) and even to offer them as gifts to less fortunate companions (H. W. Nissen and M. P. Crawford).

1. *Evolution*

Articulate language makes its appearance, after a phase of spontaneous vocalization (common to children of all cultures between six and ten or eleven months) and a phase of differentiation of phonemes by imitation (from eleven or twelve months), at the end of the sensori-motor period, with what have been called "one-word sentences" (C. Stern). These single words may express in turn desires, emotions, or observations (the verbal scheme becoming an instrument of assimilation and generalization based on the sensori-motor schemes).

From the end of the second year, two-word sentences appear, then short complete sentences without conjugation or declension, and next a gradual acquisition of grammatical structures. The syntax of children from two to four has been observed in some extremely interesting studies by R. Brown, J. Berko, and others at Harvard and S. Ervin and W. Miller at Berkeley.[23] These studies, which were inspired by Noam Chomsky's hypothesis of the structure of grammatical rules, have shown that the acquisition of syntactical rules cannot be reduced to passive imitation. It involves not only an important element of generalizing assimilation, which was more or less known, but also certain original constructions. R. Brown isolated models of these. Moreover, he has shown that reductions of adult sentences to original infantile models obey certain functional requirements, such as the conservation of a *minimum* of

[23] U. Bellugi and R. Brown, eds., *The Acquisition of Language*, Monographs of the Society for Research in Child Development, No. 92 (1964).

necessary information and the tendency to add to this *minimum*.

2. *Language and Thought*

In addition to this problem of the relationship of infantile language to linguistic theory, and to information theory, the great genetic problem raised by the development of infantile language concerns its relationship to thought, and in particular to the logical operations. Language may increase the powers of thought in range and rapidity, but it is controversial whether logico-mathematical structures are themselves essentially linguistic or nonlinguistic in nature.

As to the increasing range and rapidity of thought, thanks to language we observe in fact three differences between verbal and sensori-motor behavior. (1) Whereas sensori-motor patterns are obliged to follow events without being able to exceed the speed of the action, verbal patterns, by means of narration and evocation, can represent a long chain of actions very rapidly. (2) Sensori-motor adaptations are limited to immediate space and time, whereas language enables thought to range over vast stretches of time and space, liberating it from the immediate. (3) The third difference is a consequence of the other two. Whereas the sensori-motor intelligence proceeds by means of successive acts, step by step, thought, particularly through language, can represent simultaneously all the elements of an organized structure.

These advantages of representative thought over the sensori-motor scheme are in reality due to the semiotic function as a whole. The semiotic function detaches thought from action and is the source of representation.

Language plays a particularly important role in this formative process. Unlike images and other semiotic instruments, which are created by the individual as the need arises, language has already been elaborated socially and contains a notation for an entire system of cognitive instruments (relationships, classifications, etc.) for use in the service of thought. The individual learns this system and then proceeds to enrich it.

3. *Language and Logic*

Must we then conclude, as has been suggested, that since language possesses its own logic, this logic of language constitutes not only an essential or even a unique factor in the learning of logic (inasmuch as the child is subject to the restrictions of the linguistic group and of society in general), but is in fact the source of all logic for the whole of humanity? These views derive from the pedagogical commonsense characteristic of the sociological school of Durkheim and also the logical positivism still adhered to in many scientific circles. According to logical positivism, in fact, the logic of the logicians is itself nothing but generalized syntax and semantics (Carnap, Tarski, etc.).

We have available two sources of important information on this subject: (1) The comparison of normal children with deaf-mutes, who have not had the benefit of articulate language but are in possession of complete sensorimotor schemes, and with blind persons, whose situation is the opposite. (2) The systematic comparison of linguistic progress in the normal child with the development of intellectual operations.

The logic of deaf-mutes has been studied by M. Vincent[24] and P. Oléron,[25] in Paris, who have applied the operatory tests of the Genevan school, and by F. Affolter in Geneva. The results indicate a systematic delay in the emergence of logic in the deaf-mute. One cannot speak of deficiency as such, however, since the same stages of development are encountered, although with a delay of one to two years. Seriation and spatial operations are normal (perhaps a slight delay in the case of the former). The classifications have their customary structures and are only slightly less mobile in response to suggested changes of criteria than in hearing children. The learning of arithmetic is relatively easy. Problems of conservation (an index of reversibility) are solved with a delay of only one or two years compared with normal children. The exception is the conservation of liquids, which gives rise to special technical difficulties in the presentation of the assignment, since the subjects must be made to understand that the questions have to do with the contents of the containers and not with the containers themselves.

These results are even more significant when compared with the results obtained in studies of blind children. In studies made by Y. Hatwell, the same tests reveal a delay of up to four years or more compared with normal children, even in elementary questions dealing with relationships of order (succession, position "between," etc.). And yet in the blind children verbal seriations are normal (*A* is

[24] M. Vincent and M. Borelli, "La Naissance des opérations logiques chez des sourd-muets," *Enfance* (1951), pp. 222–238, and *Enfance* (1956), pp. 1–20.

[25] P. Oléron, "L'Acquisition des conservations et le langage," *Enfance* (1961), pp. 201–219.

smaller than B, B smaller than C, therefore . . .). But the sensory disturbance peculiar to those born blind has from the outset hampered the development of the sensori-motor schemes and slowed down general coordination. Verbal coordinations are not sufficient to compensate for this delay, and action learning is still necessary before these children develop the capacity for operations on a level with that of the normal child or the deaf-mute.

4. *Language and Operations*

The comparison of progress in language with progress in the intellectual operations requires both linguistic and psychological competence. Our collaborator, H. Sinclair, who fulfills both conditions, undertook a group of studies of which we offer one or two samples.

Two groups of children were chosen. The first was clearly preoperatory; that is, these children did not possess the least notion of conservation. The children in the second group accepted one of these notions and justified it by arguments of reversibility and compensation. Both groups were shown several pairs of objects (a large object and a small one; a group of four or five marbles and a group of two; an object that is both shorter and wider than another, etc.) and were asked to describe the pairs when one element of the pair is offered to one person and the other to a second person. This description is thus not related to a problem of conservation. The language of the two groups differs systematically. The first group uses "scalars" almost exclusively (in the linguistic sense): "this man has a big one, that man a small one; this one has a lot, that one little." The second group uses "vectors": "this man has a bigger one than the other man"; "he has more," etc. Whereas the first group describes only one dimension at a time, the second group says: "This pencil is longer and thinner," etc. In short, there is a surprising degree of correlation between the language employed and the mode of reasoning. Similarly, a second study shows a close connection between the stages of development of seriation and the structure of the terms used.

How should this relationship be interpreted? A child at the preoperatory level understands the expressions of the higher level when they are integrated into orders or assignments ("Give that man a longer pencil," etc.), but he does not use them spontaneously. If you train him to use these expressions, he learns them but with difficulty, and the training seldom influences his notions of conservation (it does in approximately one case in ten). Seriation, on the other hand, is somewhat improved by verbal training, because then the linguistic process also relates to the act of comparison and therefore to the concept itself.

These data, combined with those described on pages 87–89, indicate that language does not constitute the source of logic but is, on the contrary, structured by it. The roots of logic are to be sought in the general coordination of actions (including verbal behavior), beginning with the sensori-motor level, whose schemes are of fundamental importance. This schematism continues thereafter to develop and to structure thought, even verbal thought, in terms of the progress of actions, until the formation of the logico-mathematical operations. This is the culmination of the logic implied in the coordinations of actions, when these actions are ready to be internalized and organized into unified structures. We shall now attempt to explain this.

5. *Conclusion*

In spite of the astonishing diversity of its manifestations, the semiotic function presents a remarkable unity. Whether it is a question of deferred imitation, symbolic play, drawing, mental images and image-memories or language, this function allows the representative evocation of objects and events not perceived at that particular moment. The semiotic function makes thought possible by providing it with an unlimited field of application, in contrast to the restricted boundaries of sensori-motor action and perception. Reciprocally, it evolves under the guidance of thought, or representative intelligence. Neither imitation nor play nor drawing nor image nor language nor even memory (to which we might have attributed a capacity for spontaneous reproduction comparable to that of perception) can develop or be organized without the constant help of the structuration characteristic of intelligence. Let us now examine the evolution of intelligence, starting with the stage of representation which is the product of this semiotic function.

D*

4

THE "CONCRETE" OPERATIONS OF THOUGHT AND INTERPERSONAL RELATIONS

ONCE THE PRINCIPAL sensori-motor schemes have been developed (Chapter 1) and the semiotic function has been elaborated after the age of one and a half to two years (Chapter 3), one might expect a swift and immediate internalization of actions into operations. The establishment of the scheme of the permanent object and of the practical "group of displacements" (Chapter 1, pages 13 ff.) does, in fact, prefigure reversibility and the operatory conservations, and seems to herald their imminent appearance. But it is not until the age of seven or eight that this stage is reached, and we must understand the reasons for this delay if we are to grasp the complex nature of the operations.

I. *The Three Levels in the Transition from Action to Operation*

Actually, the existence of this delay proves that there are three levels between action and thought rather than two as some authorities[1] believed. First there is a sensori-motor level of direct action upon reality. After seven or eight there is the level of the operations, which concern transformations of reality by means of internalized actions that are grouped into coherent, reversible systems (joining and separating, etc.). Between these two, that is, between the ages of two or three and six or seven, there is another level, which is not merely transitional. Although it obviously represents an advance over direct action, in that actions are internalized by means of the semiotic function, it is also characterized by new and serious obstacles. What are these obstacles?

First we must consider the fact that a successful adaptive action is not automatically accompanied by an accurate mental representation of the situation or of the action performed. From one and a half to two, the child is in possession of a practical group of displacements which enables him to find his way about his room or his garden. He can both make detours and return to his starting point. Children of four and five often go by themselves from home to school and back every day even though the walk may be ten minutes or so in length. Yet if you ask them to

---

[1] H. Wallon, *De l'acte à la pensée* (Paris: Flammarion, 1942).

represent their path by means of little three-dimensional cardboard objects (houses, church, streets, river, squares, etc.) or to indicate the plan of the school as it is seen from the main entrance or from the side facing the river, they are unable to reconstruct the topographical relationship, even though they constantly utilize them in action. Young children's memories are in some sense motor-memories and cannot necessarily be represented in a simultaneous unified reconstruction. The first obstacle to operations, then, is the problem of mentally representing what has already been absorbed on the level of action.

Second, achieving this systematic mental representation involves constructive processes analogous to those which take place during infancy (Chapter 1, pages 13 ff.) on the sensori-motor level; namely, the transition from an initial state in which everything is centered on the child's own body and actions to a "decentered" state in which his body and actions assume their objective relationships with reference to all the other objects and events registered in the universe. This decentering, laborious enough on the level of action (where it takes at least eighteen months), is even more difficult on the level of representation, because the preschool child is involved in a much larger and more complex universe than the infant.[2]

[2] To cite only one example, it is at about four or five that a child is able to designate his right and left hands, though he may have been able to tell them apart since he reached the level of action. Yet, even though he knows how to use these notions as regards his own body, it will be two or three more years before he understands that a tree seen to the right of him when he is going one way will be on the left on the way back, or that the right hand of a person seated opposite him is on his own left; and it will take him even longer to accept the fact that an object B located be-

Third, as soon as language and the semiotic function permit not only evocation but also communication with other people (verbal or gestural language, symbolic play involving more than one participant, reciprocal imitation, etc.), the universe to be represented is no longer formed exclusively of objects (or of persons as objects), as at the sensori-motor level, but contains also subjects who have their own views of the situation that must be reconciled with those of the child, with all that this situation involves in terms of separate and multiple perspectives to be differentiated and coordinated. In other words, the decentering which is a prerequisite for the formation of the operations applies not only to a physical universe (and the physical universe is already substantially more complex than the sensori-motor universe) but also necessarily to an interpersonal or social universe. Unlike most actions, the operations always involve a possibility of exchange, of interpersonal as well as personal coordination, and this cooperative aspect constitutes an indispensable condition for the objectivity, internal coherence (that is, their "equilibrium"), and universality of these operatory structures.

The decentering of cognitive constructions necessary for the development of the operations is inseparable from the decentering of affective and social constructions. But the term "social" must not be thought of in the narrow sense of educational, cultural, or moral transmission alone; rather, it covers an interpersonal process of socialization which is at once cognitive, affective, and moral. This process may be traced in broad outline—but we must not forget that the optimal conditions are in fact unattainable and

---

tween A and C can be at the same time to the right of A and to the left of C.

that this evolution is subject to considerable fluctuation, teaching both its cognitive and its affective aspects.

In this chapter, then, we shall consider the very long period between two or three and eleven or twelve, rather than separating a preoperatory stage up to about seven or eight from the later stage of concrete operations. The first of these two great phases, although it lasts four or five years, is in fact only a time of organization and preparation comparable to Stages 1 to 3 (or 4) of sensori-motor development (Chapter 1, pages 6 ff.), whereas the period between seven or eight and eleven or twelve marks the completion of the concrete operations, comparable to Stages 4 or 5 and 6 in the formation of the sensori-motor schemes. After this, a new operatory period—characteristic of pre-adolescence and attaining its point of equilibrium at about fourteen or fifteen—makes it possible to complete the limited and partially lacunary constructions characteristic of the concrete operations.

II. *The Genesis of the "Concrete" Operations*

The operations, such as the union of two classes (fathers united with mothers constitute parents) or the addition of two numbers, are *actions* characterized by their very great generality since the acts of uniting, arranging in order, etc., enter into all coordinations of particular actions. They are also reversible (the opposite of uniting is separating, the opposite of addition is subtraction, etc.). Furthermore, they are never isolated but are always capable of being coordinated into overall systems (for instance, a classification, the sequence of numbers, etc.). Finally they are not peculiar to a given individual; they are common to all individuals on the same mental level. And they enter into both the individual's private reasoning and his cognitive exchanges, for cognitive exchanges also bring together information and place it in relation to other information, introduce reciprocities, etc. In short, all this involves operations comparable to those which each individual uses for himself.

The operations consist of reversible transformations. The reversibility may be of two kinds: inversions, where $+A$ is reversed by $-A$, and reciprocity, where $A < B$ is reciprocated by $B < A$. Now, a reversible transformation does not change everything at the same time; otherwise it would be irreversible. An operatory transformation therefore always leaves some feature of the system constant. The constant invariant in a system of transformations is what up to now we have used to label a scheme of conservation (Chapter 1, pages 13 ff., Chapter 2, pages 43 ff., etc.); thus the scheme of the permanent object is the constant feature of the practical group of displacements since a displacement does not change the properties of the object that is moved. Notions of conservation may therefore serve as psychological indication of the completion of an operatory structure.

1. *Notions of Conservation*

The clearest indication of the existence of a preoperatory period corresponding to the second of the levels distinguished in the preceding section is the absence of notions of conservation until about the age of seven or eight. Let us reexamine the experiment relating to the conservation of liquids[3] in which the contents of glass *A* were poured into a narrower glass *B* or a wider glass *C*. Two facts are particularly noteworthy in the judgments of four- to six-year-olds who think that the liquid increases or decreases in quantity. First, the young subjects seem to reason only about states or static configurations, overlooking transformations: the water in *B* is higher than it was in *A*; therefore it has increased in quantity, regardless of the fact that it is the same water that has merely been poured from one container to another. Second, the transformation, although the child is perfectly well aware of it, is not conceived as a reversible movement from one state to another, changing the form but leaving the quantity constant. It is viewed as a particular action, a "pouring," situated on a level other than that of physical phenomena and assumed to have results that are literally incalculable, that is, non-deductible in their external application. However, at the level of concrete operations, after seven or eight, the child says: "It is the same water," "It has only been poured," "Nothing has been taken away or added" (simple or additive identities): "You can put the water in *B* back into *A* where it was before" (reversibility by inversion); or, particularly, "The water is higher, but the glass is narrower, so it's the same amount" (compensation or reversibility by reciprocal relationship). The states are henceforth subordinated to the transformations, and these transformations, being de-centered from the action of the subject, become reversible and account both for the changes in their compensated variations and for the constant implied by reversibility.

[3] Jean Piaget and Alina Szeminska, *The Child's Conception of Number* (New York: Humanities Press, 1952; London: Routledge and Kegan Paul, 1952).

These facts may serve as an example of the general pattern for the acquisition of every notion of conservation beginning with preoperatory reactions of non-conservation. There are many specific varieties of conservation following this pattern. The child discovers the conservation of substance at seven or eight, as is clear from his judgment of changes in shape of a lump of clay.[4] He discovers the conservation of weight at nine or ten, and the conservation of volume at eleven or twelve (measurement of displaced water when the object is immersed). The conservation of length (comparison of a straight line with another line of the same length which is first straight, then broken; or of two congruent straight rods, one of which is moved away from the other), the conservation of surfaces or volumes (by displacement of elements), or the conservation of wholes after the changing of spatial arrangements—all show that at the preoperatory levels the reactions are centered on perceptual or imagined configurations, while at the operatory levels the reactions are based on identity or reversibility by inversion or reciprocity.[5]

[4] Jean Piaget and Bärbel Inhelder, *Le Développement des quantités physiques chez l'enfant* (Neuchâtel: Delachaux et Niestlé, 1941; 2nd ed., 1962).

[5] These results, which have been confirmed by writers in several countries, were established by us not only by means of primarily qualitative interrogations and statistical verification, but by other means as well. One of us used these questions "longitudinally"; that is, with the same children but at repeated intervals. This showed, on the one hand, that a "natural" and very gradual process was involved (without regression to outgrown levels) and confirmed, on the other, that the three arguments used to justify the conservations are interdependent. For example, identity does not necessarily precede reversibility, but results from it implicitly or explicitly. A series of experiments was also under-

2. *The Concrete Operations*

The operations involved in these problems are called "concrete" because they relate directly to objects and not yet to verbally stated hypotheses, as is the case with the propositional operations that we shall study in Chapter 5. Concrete operations provide a transition between schemes of action and the general logical structures involving both a combinatorial system and a "group" structure coordinating the two possible forms of reversibility. Concrete operations are already coordinated into overall structures, but these structures are weak and permit only step-by-step reasoning, for lack of generalized combinations. These structures include classifications, seriations, correspondences (one to one or one to several), matrices or double-entry tables, etc. The essence of these structures, called "groupings," is to constitute progressive logical sequences involving various combinations of operations. These operations can be direct (for example, a class united with its complementary class A' gives a total class B; then $B + B' = C$, etc.), inverse ($B - A' = A$), identical ($+ A - A = 0$), or tautological ($A + A = A$). Notice these operations are only partly associative: $(A + A') + B' = A + (A' + B')$, but $(A + A) - A \neq A + (A - A)$.

---

taken to analyze factors intervening in the discovery of the conservations; these involved training in the fundamental mechanisms of reversibility, identity, and compensation, succession of strategies from the simplest to the most complex, etc. In these cases one observes the use of regulations (with loops and feedbacks) effecting the transition to the operation, although these short-term learning processes are insufficient to give rise to the operatory structures or to achieve those closed systems which make possible a method that may properly be called deductive.

It is possible to trace on the different preoperatory levels the successive beginnings of what will become the additive and multiplicative "groupings" of classes and relations,[6] with the achievement of a completely reversible mobility and consequently of coherent deductive composition.

3. *Seriation*

A good example of this constructive process is seriation, which consists in arranging elements according to increasing or decreasing size. There are intimations of this operation on the sensori-motor level when the child of one and a half or two builds, for example, a tower of two or three blocks whose dimensional differences are immediately perceptible. Later, when the subject must seriate ten markers whose differences in length are so small that they must be compared two at a time, the following stages are observed: first the markers are separated into groups of two or three (one short, one long, etc.), each seriated with itself but incapable of being coordinated into a single series; next, a construction by empirical groping in which the child keeps rearranging the order until he finally recognizes he has it right; finally, a systematic method that consists in seeking first the smallest element, then the smallest of those left over, and so on. In this case the method is operatory, for a given element E is understood in advance to be simulta-

[6] From the logical point of view; the "grouping" is an integrated structure with limited arrangements (by contiguity or step-by-step composition), related to the "group" but without complete associativity (cf. a "groupoid") and close to the "network" but only in the form of a semi-lattice. Its logical structure has been formalized by J. B. Grize (*Etudes d'épistémologie génétique,* Vol. 2) and by G. G. Granger (*Logique et analyse,* 8th year, 1965).

neously larger than the preceding elements ($E > D, C, B,$ A) and smaller than the following elements ($E < F, G,$ etc.), which is a form of reversibility by reciprocity. But above all, at the moment when the structure arrives at completion, there immediately results a mode of deductive composition hitherto unknown: transitivity, i.e., if $A < B$ and $B < C$ then $A < C$. The child's understanding of transitivity may be tested by having subjects compare A and B and then B and C perceptually, but then they must deduce A's relation to C, without comparing the two, which preoperatory subjects refuse to do.

From this operatory seriation, acquired at about seven, follow one-to-one serial correspondences (matching to "little men" of various sizes, a series of canes of various sizes and a set of knapsacks likewise seriable). Two-dimensional seriations also become possible (for example, arranging on a double-entry table leaves from trees varying both in size and in depth of color). These systems are also acquired at seven or eight.

4. *Classification*

Classification is another fundamental grouping whose roots can be traced back to the sensori-motor schemes. When children from three to twelve are given a set of objects and instructed to "put the things that are alike together," their sortings can be divided into three basic stages.[7] The youngest subjects begin with "figural collections"; that is, they arrange the objects not only according to their individual similarities and differences, but also jux-

[7] Bärbel Inhelder and Jean Piaget, *The Early Growth of Logic in the Child: Classification and Seriation* (London: Routledge and Kegan Paul, 1964).

tapose them spatially in rows, squares, circles, etc., so that the collection itself forms a figure in space. This figure serves as a perceptual or imagined expression of the "extension" of the class. The second stage is the stage of non-figural collections; the set is divided into small groups of elements each without any particular spatial form and these groups themselves can even be differentiated into subgroups. The classification now seems rational (after five and a half or six), but upon analysis it still betrays lacunae in "extension." If, for example, in a group B of twelve flowers within which there is a subgroup A of six primroses, you ask the child to show first the flowers B and next the primroses A, he responds correctly, because he can designate the whole B and the part A. However, if you ask him, "Are there more flowers or more primroses?" he is unable to respond according to the inclusion $A < B$, because if he thinks of the part A, the whole B ceases to be conserved as a unit, and the part A is henceforth comparable only to its complementary A'. He may reply, therefore, "the same," or, if there are a clear majority of primroses in the set, he may say that there are more primroses. The understanding of the relative sizes of an included class to the entire class is achieved at about eight and marks the achievement of a genuine operatory classification.[8]

[8] To this are related the double classifications (double-entry tables or matrices) which appear at the same point in the child's development; for example, being able to classify red or white squares and circles in four compartments arranged according to two dimensions. These structures have been used as tests of intelligence, but insufficient care has been taken to distinguish operatory solutions from merely perceptual solutions based upon figural symmetries. Work has also been done on changes of criteria in

5. *Number*

The construction of whole numbers occurs in the child in close connection with the construction of seriations and class inclusions. One must not think that a young child understands number simply because he can count verbally. In his mind numerical evaluation is for a long time linked with the spatial arrangement of the elements, in close analogy with "figural collections" (see the preceding section). The experiment described in Chapter 3, pages 78–79, shows this clearly: if you space out the elements of one of two rows initially aligned optically, the subject ceases to accept their numerical equivalence. Naturally, there can be no question of operatory numbers before the existence of a conservation of numerical groups independent of spatial arrangement.

Having said this, one might assume, according to set theory and as the logicians Frege, Whitehead, and Russell hold, that number proceeds from a term-to-term correspondence between two classes or two sets; that is, two sets have the same number if their members can be put in one-to-one correspondence. But there are two forms of correspondences: the qualified correspondences based on the resemblance of elements (for example, a nose for a nose, a forehead for a forehead, etc., as in the correspondence between a model and its copy), and the random or "one-to-one" correspondences. It is the random correspondences that lead to number, for they already imply numerical

---

classifications; that is, the anticipatory and retroactive regulations culminating in reversible mobility.

unity. Number must still be explained genetically, however; otherwise a vicious circle results.

Number, then, results primarily from an ignoring of differential qualities which renders every individual element equivalent to every other element: one orange is equivalent to one tree is equivalent to one person as far as number is concerned. Once this is established, sets are classifiable according to inclusion ($<$): $1 < (1 + 1) < (1 + 1 + 1)$, etc. But they are also seriable ($\rightarrow$), and the only way to tell them apart and not to count the same one twice in these inclusions is to serialize them in space or in time:[9] one and then another one and then another one; $1 \rightarrow 1 \rightarrow 1$, etc. Number thus appears as a synthesis of seriation and inclusion: $\{[(1) \rightarrow 1] \rightarrow 1\} \rightarrow$ etc. This is why it is formed in close connection with these two groupings (see Sections 3 and 4, above), but as an original and new synthesis. Here again, child psychology sheds light on questions that would remain obscure without the genetic perspective. A number of studies, both experimental and theoretical (logical formalization), have been carried out with this in mind.[10]

[9] That is, not according to the relation "greater than" but according to the relations "before" and "after."

[10] For example, P. Greco, who studied the later stages in the construction of number, showed that numerical synthesis of classes and serial order occurs only gradually for numbers higher than 7–8 or 14–15. Thus one can speak of a progressive arithmetization of the numerical series. From the point of view of logical formalization, J. B. Grize provided a coherent explanation of the synthesis in question by showing how the limitations inherent in the groupings disappear as soon as all the groupings of classes and relations are fused into a single group. (*Etudes d'épistémologie*, Vols. 13 and 15, 1961–1962, Paris: Presses Universitaires de France.)

6. *Space*

The operatory structures discussed above relate to discrete objects and are based on the differences and similarities or equivalences between the elements. There is also a group of structures isomorphic to those just discussed; they relate to continuous objects and are based on proximities and separations. (The segments of a single line belong together because they are adjacent and form a continuous straight line and segments are parts of separate lines if they are disconnected.) These operations are called "infralogical" because they relate to another level of reality, and not because they develop earlier. They are constructed parallel to and in synchronization with the logico-arithmetic operations, especially in the case of spatial operations (as well as in the case of temporal operations, cinematic operations, etc.). A striking example is spatial measurement,[11] which develops independently of number but in close isomorphism with it (with a time lag of about six months, because in continuous space unity is not given in advance). Measurement of the length of a line begins, in fact, with a dividing up of continuous space into segments and an interlocking of the parts in a manner analogous to the inclusion of classes. But, in order to establish and utilize this unity, one of the segments must be taken as a unit and applied successively to the whole by means of ordered displacement (that is, without overlapping, etc.), which corresponds to a form of seriation. Thus measurement appears as a synthesis of displacement and parti-

[11] Jean Piaget, Bärbel Inhelder, and Alina Szeminska, *The Child's Conception of Geometry* (New York: Basic Books, 1960; London: Routledge and Kegan Paul, 1960).

tive addition in the same sense as number is a synthesis of seriation and inclusion.

But measurement is only a particular instance of spatial operations. If we consider these as a whole in relation to the child, we observe a situation of great general and theoretical interest. Historically, scientific geometry began with Euclidean metric geometry; then came projective geometry, and finally topology. Theoretically, however, topology constitutes a general foundation from which both projective space and the general metrics from which Euclidean metrics proceeds can be derived in a parallel manner. What is remarkable is that the line of development from the preoperatory intuitions through the spatial operations in the child is much closer to the theoretical order than to the historical genealogy. The topological structures of ordinal partition (proximities, separations, envelopment, openness and closedness, coordination of proximities in linear, bidimensional, or tridimensional order, etc.) precede the others in a rather clear-cut manner. These basic structures then give rise simultaneously and in parallel fashion to the projective structures (rectilinearity, coordination of view points, etc.) and the metrical structures (displacements, measurement, coordinates or systems of reference, as an extension of measurement to two or three dimensions). (See also Chapter 3, pages 63 ff.)

7. *Time and Speed*

Finally, let us review the operations involved in the structuration of speed and of time.[12] In accordance with

[12] Jean Piaget, *The Child's Conception of Movement and Speed* (New York: Basic Books, 1969; London: Routledge and Kegan Paul, 1969), and Jean Piaget, *Le Développement de la notion du temps chez l'enfant* (Paris: Presses Universitaires de France, 1946).

the initial primacy of topological and ordinal structures, the notion of speed does not make its first appearance in a metrical form ($V = s/t$), which is not arrived at until ten or eleven, but in an ordinal form. One moving object is faster than another if it overtakes it; that is, if it was behind it at a previous moment and is in front of it at a later moment. At a preoperatory level the child generally considers only the points of arrival (and fails to understand that more speed is required just to catch up and arrive at the same time); then he structures anticipated overtakings as well as observed overtakings in an operatory manner; later he notices the increasing or decreasing size of the intervals (hyperordinal level); and finally comes to relate duration with distance covered.

The notion of time is based, in its completed form, on three kinds of operations: (1) a seriation of events, which constitutes the order of temporal succession; (2) an inclusion of the intervals between events occurring at a certain point of time, which is the source of the notion of duration; and (3) temporal metrics (already at work in the system of musical units, well before any scientific elaboration) analogous to spatial metrics. However, whereas the ordinal structuration of speeds is independent of duration (but not, of course, of temporal order), duration, like simultaneity, depends on speed. Indeed, the preceding operations (1–3) remain independent of the greater or lesser rapidity of the passage of time and teach the subject nothing about the cadence of this passage itself,[13] because the cadence depends on the physical or psychological

[13] Indeed, if one hour measured by the clock lasted ten times longer or one tenth as long, operations 1–3 would give the same results for the same events.

content of the duration, from which the duration is insep-arable. The child begins to judge duration only in terms of this content, forgetting speed (as we often do ourselves in intuitive evaluations). Thus the child estimates that a moving object has been in motion longer if it has gone farther. Later, this content is seen in relation to speed, which then constitutes time as an objective relation and provides a grasp of the passage of time as such. This is evident in the measurement of time (the speed of the movement of the clock). In young subjects, however, such points of reference are useless, for these children im-agine that the hands of a watch or the sand in an hourglass moves at variable rates of speed depending on the content to be measured.

III. *Representation of the Universe: Causality and Chance*

In association with the operatory nucleus of thought there develop a great number of activities structured at various degrees according to the ease with which they succeed in assimilating reality. Causality and chance are the two es-sential poles between which they are distributed.

After three or thereabouts, the child begins asking him-self and those around him questions, of which the most frequently noticed are the "why" questions. By studying what the child asks "why" about one can begin to see what kind of answers or solutions the child expects to re-ceive. It is obviously necessary to use the same or similar questions to interrogate other children.

A first general observation is that the child's whys bear witness to an intermediate precausality between the efficient cause and the final cause. Specifically, these questions seek reasons for phenomena which we see as fortuitous but which in the child arouse a need for a finalist explanation. "Why are there two Mount Salèves, a big one and a little one?" asked a six-year-old boy. To which almost all his contemporaries, when asked the same question, replied, "One for big trips and another for small trips."

One of us once tried to describe the principal characteristics of this infantile preoperatory precausality.[14] In addition to an almost universal finalism, he found a "realism" due to a lack of differentiation between the psychical and the physical. Names are attached physically to things; dreams are little material tableaux which you contemplate in your bedroom; thought is a kind of voice ("the mouth in the back of my head that talks to the mouth in front"). Animism springs from the same lack of differentiation, but in the opposite direction: everything that is in movement is alive and conscious, the wind knows that it blows, the sun that it moves, etc. To questions of origin, so important to children in that they are related to the problem of the birth of babies, the young subjects reply with a systematic artificialism: men dug the lake, put water into it, and all this water comes from fountains and pipes. The stars "were born when we were born," says a boy of six, "because before that there was no need for sunlight," and the sun started as a little ball which somebody threw into the air

[14] Jean Piaget, *The Child's Conception of Physical Causality* (London: Routledge and Kegan Paul, 1930).

and which grew, for it is possible to be both living and manufactured, as babies are.[15]

Interestingly enough, this precausality is close to the initial sensori-motor forms of causality which we called "magical-phenomenalist" in Chapter 1. Like those, it results from a systematic assimilation of physical processes to the child's own action, an assimilation which sometimes leads to quasi-magical attitudes (for instance, many subjects between four and six believe that the moon follows them or even that they force it to follow them). But, just as sensori-motor precausality makes way (after Stages 4 to 6 of infancy) for an objectified and spatialized causality, so representative precausality, which is essentially an assimilation to action, is gradually, at the level of concrete operations, transformed into a rational causality by assimilation no longer to the child's own actions in their egocentric orientation but to the operations as general coordinations of actions.

A good example of operatory causality is infantile atomism as it is derived from additive operations and from the conservation that results from them. In connection

[15] Precausality has been studied by a number of English-speaking writers, of whom some agreed and some violently disagreed with these interpretations. After that there was silence until two Canadians, M. Laurendeau and A. Pinard (*La Pensée causale,* Paris: Presses Universitaires de France, 1962), reviewed both the data (on a large statistical scale) and the methods used. Generally speaking, the data were found to be the same. But different methods of analysis had been applied. The writers who favored precausality had analyzed their results child by child, as we did, whereas those opposed had analyzed their results object by object, without taking individual reactions into account.

with experiments in conservation, we once asked children from five to twelve what happens after lumps of sugar are dissolved in a glass of water.[16] For children up to about seven, the dissolved sugar disappears and its taste vanishes like a mere odor; for children seven to eight its substance is retained without either its weight or its volume. After nine or ten, conservation of weight is present, and after eleven or twelve, there is also conservation of volume (recognizable in the fact that the level of the water, which is slightly raised when the sugar is added, does not return to its initial level after the sugar is dissolved). The child explains this triple conservation (which is parallel to what one finds in the case of changes of shape in a lump of clay) by the hypothesis that, in the act of melting, the grains of sugar become very small and invisible, and thus conserve, first their substance without weight or volume, then substance plus weight, and finally all three. Thus the sum of these elementary grains equals first the total substance, then the weight, and then the volume of the lumps of sugar before they were dissolved. This is a fine example of a causal explanation by the projection into reality of an operatory composition.

The obstacle to these operatory forms of causality is that reality resists deduction and involves a greater or lesser element of uncertainty. The child, however, does not grasp the notion of chance or of irreversible mixing until he is in possession of reversible operations to serve him as references. Once these reversible operations have been formed, he then understands the irreversible as a resistance to operatory deductibility.

[16] Jean Piaget and Bärbel Inhelder, *Le Développement des quantités physiques chez l'enfant.*

A simple experiment which we made[17] in this connection consisted in presenting a box containing ten white beads on one side and ten black beads on the other, grouped respectively in little compartments. The idea was to anticipate the gradual mixing of the beads when the box was rocked and the very low probability that with further rocking the white beads would be separated from the black beads. At the preoperatory level finality prevails over fortuitousness: each bead will return to its place, according to the child of four to six. When he observes the mixing, he says the beads will become unmixed, or else that the black beads will trade places with the whites in a kind of regular and rhythmic square dance. After eight or nine, however, there is anticipation of mixing and awareness of the improbability that the beads will return to their initial position.

Chance is at first conceived only in a negative sense, as an obstacle to deductibility. The child later comes to assimilate the element of chance to the operation by understanding that although he cannot foresee the outcome of individual events, he can anticipate the outcome of a large number of instances taken together. Thus the notion of probability as a ratio of favorable cases to possible cases is gradually established. But the completion of the notion of probability presupposes a combinatorial system—a structure which will not be elaborated until after the age of eleven or twelve (Chapter 5, page 144).

[17] Jean Piaget and Bärbel Inhelder, *La Genèse de l'idée de hasard chez l'enfant* (Paris: Presses Universitaires de France, 1951).

IV. *Social and Affective Interactions*

We have just described the cognitive aspect of the developmental process which connects the structures of the initial sensori-motor level with those of the level of concrete operations that is reached between seven and eleven. First, however, there is a preoperatory period (two to seven) characterized by systematic assimilation to the child's own action (symbolic play, non-conservations, precausality, etc.) which constitutes an obstacle to, as well as a preparation for, operatory assimilation. The affective and social development of the child follows the same general process, since the affective, social, and cognitive aspects of behavior are in fact inseparable. As we have already seen (Chapter 1, pages 21 ff.), affectivity constitutes the energetics of behavior patterns, whose structures correspond to cognitive functions, and even though the energetics may not explain the structuration, or the structuration the energetics, neither one can function without the other.

1. *Evolution*

The appearance of representation, as a result of semiotic function, is just as important for the development of affectivity and social relations as it is for the development of the cognitive functions. During the sensori-motor period an object can be affectively significant only while the child is in direct contact with it. It can be brought back after momentary separation but it cannot be evoked during the separation. With the mental image, the memory of evocation, symbolic play, and language, however, the affective object may be present and active even in its physical absence. This fundamental fact results in the formation of new affects in the form of lasting sympathies or antipathies toward other people and of a permanent awareness and valorization of oneself as regards the ego.

Thus a series of new phenomena emerge whose peak comes at about three with what Bühler has called the crisis of opposition and is marked by a need for assertion and independence and by rivalries of all kinds, Oedipal and otherwise, in relation to elders. This is expressed in the elaborations of symbolic play in its affective aspects as well as in effective and non-playful behavior. This growing realization of the self, which constitutes a valorization much more than an introspective discovery, leads the child to oppose other people. However, since it is fundamentally concerned with valorization, it also brings the child to try to win other people's affection and esteem.[18]

[18] G. Guex, "Les Conditions intellectuelles et affectives de l'Oedipe," *Revue française de psychanalyse,* No. 2 (1949), pp. 257–276. According to Guex, the establishment of object relations at the sensori-motor level is due primarily to a need for security, whereas from three to five the dominant need is to win the other's esteem. However, Guex speaks here of autonomy and is amazed to see it appear before cooperation, which begins so clearly at seven or eight (that is, in close association with the development of the concrete operations, for reasons we have already mentioned and will mention again). In reality the crisis of opposition is by no means characterized by autonomy in the sense in which it appears at the age of eight; that is, by a submission of the self to rules ("nomia") which the child sets himself ("auto") or which he works out freely in cooperation with his peers. It is characterized by independence ("anomia" rather than autonomy) and by opposition; that is, by the complex and contradictory situation in which the self wants to be at the same time free of and esteemed by the other.

E

2. The Problem

This dialectical situation, still unstable and equivocal, dominates early infancy and social behavior at that stage, which explains the controversy and occasional breakdown of communication between writers who placed particular emphasis on one or the other pole of the social life characteristic of this period.

Let us note first that the term "social" corresponds to two very distinct realities in the affective sense, as has already been made clear in the cognitive sense. First, there is the relationship between the child and the adult which is the source of educational and verbal transmissions of cultural elements in the cognitive sense, and of specific sentiments, in particular, the moral sentiments (see below, pages 122 ff.) in the affective sense. Second, there are also the social relations among the children themselves, and in part between the children and the adults, but as a continuous and constructive process of reciprocal socialization and no longer simply a unilateral transmission.

It is this process of socialization which has constituted a problem. For some writers (Bühler,[19] Grünbaum, Buytendijk,[20] Wallon,[21] and his follower Zazzo[22]), the child presents a *maximum* of social interactions or at least of social interdependence during early childhood (our pre-

[19] Charlotte Bühler, *Kindheit und Jugend* (3rd ed.; Leipzig: Hirzel, 1931).

[20] F. J. J. Buytendijk, *Wesen und Sinn des Spiels* (Berlin: Wolff, 1934).

[21] H. Wallon, "L'Étude psychologique et sociologique de l'enfant," *Cahiers internationaux de sociologie,* III (1947), 3–23.

[22] R. Zazzo, *Les Jumeaux* (Paris: Presses Universitaires de France, 1960).

operatory level). After that, he achieves an individualized personality by a kind of retreat or liberation from these initial interdependences. For other writers, including ourselves, the process of socialization is progressive rather than regressive. In spite of the appearance of individuality tending toward autonomy, the child of seven and over is more socialized than the self of early childhood which is in interdependence with others. The initial social interdependencies before seven actually attest to a *minimum* of socialization, because they are insufficiently structured (the internal structure of the relations being much more important here than the overall phenomenology adopted).

If we reexamine this disagreement today, it seems quite obvious that the opposing sides are in fact saying almost the same thing. The difference is in the terminology and not in the conclusions reached. It is important, therefore, to concentrate on a relational rather than a conceptual analysis and to distinguish the points of view of the subject and of the observer in such a way that certain connections may be interpreted both as social interdependences and as inadequate instruments of socialization.

3. *Socialization*

Since it is widely accepted that cognitive and affective or social development are inseparable and parallel, the surest course is to turn to studies of intellectual attitudes at the preoperatory level. In this respect, precausality (see above, pages 110 ff.) constitutes a remarkable instance of a situation in which the subject believes he has grasped the external and objective mechanisms of reality, whereas from the observer's point of view it is clear that he is merely assimilating them to a certain number of subjective characteristics of his own action. What is obvious in the case of precausality is just as true, though sometimes less apparent, of the non-conservations and all the preoperatory reactions. Generally speaking, the fundamental difference between the preoperatory and the operatory levels is that at the preoperatory level assimilation to the child's own action prevails, whereas the operatory level is dominated by assimilation to the general coordinations of action, and therefore to the operations.

Thus we see from the outset the possible analogy with the phases of the process of socialization. The general coordination of actions which characterizes the functional nucleus of the operations includes interpersonal as well as intrapersonal actions. It is meaningless, therefore, to wonder whether it is the cognitive cooperation (or cooperations) which engender the individual operations or the other way around. It is at the stage of concrete operations that new interpersonal relations of a cooperative nature are established, and there is no reason why these should be limited to cognitive exchanges.

It is highly probable, then, that the social exchanges characteristic of the preoperatory level are precooperative; that is, at once social from the point of view of the subject and centered upon the child and his own activity from the point of view of the observer. This is precisely what one of us meant by "infantile egocentrism." But, as we have mentioned (Chapter 3, page 61, note 6), this term has often been misunderstood, although we have always insisted on its epistemological meaning (difficulty in understanding differences in points of view between the speakers and therefore in decentration) rather than on its popular or "moral" meaning.

The facts are clear today in three areas: games with rules, group actions, and verbal exchanges.

i) Games with rules are social institutions in that they remain the same as they are transmitted from one generation to the next and are independent of the will of the individuals who participate in them. Some of these games are transmitted with the participation of adults, but others are specifically infantile, like the game of marbles, which the boys of Geneva play until they are eleven or twelve. The second kind, which are both play and exclusively "children's property," are the most favorable for the advancement of social life among children.

Games of marbles, after the age of seven, are well structured. There is a common observance of the rules, which are known to the players; mutual surveillance to make sure the rules are observed; and, above all, a collective spirit of honest competition, so that some win and others lose according to accepted rules. The play of younger subjects is quite different. First, because the set of rules is complex, a younger subject can retain only part of the rules he has learned from an older child. What he has learned may not correspond to what another young child has acquired. Second, everyone plays the game as he understands it, without much concern for or checking up on what the others are doing. Last, and most significant, nobody loses and everybody wins at the same time, for the purpose is to have fun by playing for oneself while being stimulated by the group and participating in a collective ambiance. There is, then, a total lack of differentiation between social behavior and concentration on individual action. True cooperation does not exist yet, even on the level of play.

ii) In an interesting study on cooperative work in children of different ages, R. Froyland Nielsen[23] observed spontaneous activities and also subjected the children to arrangements calling for a minimum of organization: working in pairs on desks that were too small, having only one pencil to draw with or pencils that were tied together, utilizing a common medium, etc. Thus she obtained two kinds of results. On the one hand, she observed a more or less regular development from solitary work to collaboration. (The later solitary work of adults does not have the same non-intentional and unconscious significance as the solitary activity of children, who, while working independently, feel that they are in communion and in synergy with their neighbors without necessarily paying attention to their specific activity.) On the other hand, Nielsen observed the children's initial difficulty in finding (even in seeking) modes of collaboration, as if collaboration did not constitute a specific end that must be pursued for its own sake.

iii) The studies one of us conducted on the functions of language in exchanges among children led to similar results. These, although they gave rise to the other studies mentioned, have, however, been far more controversial. The fact is that the speech of subjects between four and six (observed in situations in which children work, play, and speak freely) is not intended to provide information, ask questions, etc. (that is, it is not socialized language), but consists rather of monologues or "collective monologues" in the course of which everyone talks to himself

[23] R. Froyland Nielsen, *Le Développement de la sociabilité chez l'enfant* (Neuchâtel: Delachaux et Niestlé, 1951).

without listening to the others (that is, egocentric language).

The percentage of egocentric remarks, it has been shown, depends on the milieu. In exchanges between parents and children, D. and R. Katz found very few such remarks, whereas Leuzinger, who was both the mother and the schoolteacher of the child studied, observed more of them in the home than in school and more with an adult than among children (a matter of directive or non-directive educational technique). N. Isaacs observed few such remarks during pleasant schoolwork, but many more in play (which is quite consistent with what we have seen in connection with symbolic play).[24]

It is essential not to limit oneself to the spontaneous remarks of children in general—experience shows that interpreting them is not always easy—but, as one of us has already done, to make a thorough analysis of the success a child has in getting another child to do something by means of language, as when one child tries to explain something to another or in discussions among children. In both situations, one sees the systematic difficulty children have in taking the point of view of the other, in making him grasp the desired information, and in modifying his initial comprehension. It is only after long training that the

[24] As for the interpretation of egocentric language, L. S. Vygotsky (*Thought and Language,* New York: Wiley, 1962), who observed the same phenomenon in the U.S.S.R., interprets it as the functional infantile equivalent and the source of the internal language of the adult; that is, as a personal, but not necessarily egocentric, use of speech. This interpretation is acceptable, provided one stipulates that it does not exclude egocentrism (in the specific sense indicated).

child reaches the point (at the operatory stage) where he speaks no longer for himself but from the point of view of the other. In his study on egocentric language, Zazzo concluded that in situations like these the child does not speak "for himself" but "according to himself"; that is, on the basis of his limitations as well as his possibilities. We can only concur. But we must repeat our earlier remarks that, from his own point of view, the subject speaks for the other and not for himself, but, looked at from the vantage point of the observer, who is comparing the child's present performance with what he will be able to accomplish, the subject speaks for himself and fails to establish a cooperative contact.

V. *Moral Feelings and Judgments*

The affective relationship beween the child and his parents, or the adults who play the parental role, engenders the specific moral feelings forced upon one by one's conscience. Freud popularized the notion of a "superego," or the internalization of the affective image of the father or parents, which becomes a source of duties, coercive models, remorse, and sometimes even of self-punishment. But this conception is older than Freud; it can be found, remarkably developed, in the work of Baldwin. This writer explained the formation of the self in terms of imitation (since imitation is necessary to provide first a complete image of the child's own body, then a comparison between the general reactions of the other and the self). Further, Baldwin showed that beyond a certain point, which is reached because of conflicts of will and the superior general powers of the adult, the self of the parents can no longer be imitated immediately, and thus becomes an "ideal self" which is a source of coercive models and of moral conscience.

1. *The Genesis of Duty*

Bovet [25] furnished a more detailed and accurate analysis of this process. According to him, the formation of the sense of obligation is subject to two conditions: (1) the intervention of orders given from the outside, that is, orders of indeterminate time span (don't tell lies, etc.); and (2) the acceptance of these orders, which presupposes the existence of a sentiment *sui generis* on the part of the person who receives the order toward the person who gives it (for the child does not accept orders from just anyone, for example a younger brother or sister or an unimportant person). According to Bovet, this sentiment is one of respect and consists of affection and fear. Affection alone could not suffice to produce obligation, and fear alone provokes only a physical or self-interested submission, but respect involves both affection and the fear associated with the position of the inferior in relation to the superior, and therefore suffices to determine the acceptance of orders and consequently the sense of obligation.[26]

[25] P. Bovet, "Les Conditions de l'obligation de conscience," *Année psychologique,* 1912.

[26] This analysis, based on child psychology, is opposed to the theories of both Kant and Durkheim. Kant saw respect as a unique sentiment not attached to a person per se, but aroused by a person to the degree that he embodies or represents moral law. Durkheim thought along the same lines, but replaced "law" with "society." For both, respect was a result of obligation, and subsequent to it, whereas for Bovet it is its prerequisite. There is no

E*

The sentiment described by Bovet constitutes only one of two possible forms of respect. We shall call it "unilateral," since it binds an inferior to a superior who is regarded as such, and shall distinguish it from "mutual respect," which is based on reciprocity of esteem. Unilateral respect, if it is indeed the source of the sense of duty, begets in the young child a morality of obedience which is characterized primarily by a *heteronomy* that declines later to make way, at least partially, for the autonomy characteristic of mutual respect.[27]

2. *Heteronomy*

Heteronomy is expressed by a number of affective reactions and by certain remarkable structures peculiar to moral judgment before the age of seven or eight.

From the affective point of view it should first be noted (as one of us and several collaborators of Lewin have done) that the power of orders is initially dependent upon the physical presence of the person who gives them. In his absence the law loses its force and its violation is accompanied only by a momentary uneasiness.

Later this power becomes permanent and the process of systematic-assimilation occurs which psychoanalysts refer to when they speak of identification with the parental image or with authority figures. But the submission cannot

---

question that Bovet is right insofar as the child is concerned. The child does not respect his father as a representative of the law or the social group but as a superior individual who is the source of compulsions and laws.

[27] Jean Piaget, *The Moral Judgment of the Child* (London: Routledge and Kegan Paul, 1932; Glencoe, Ill.: The Free Press, 1948).

be complete, and parental or authority figures give rise to ambivalence. The elements that make up respect become dissociated and the dissociation leads to a mixture of affection and hostility, sympathy and aggression, jealousy, etc. It is probable that the feelings of guilt that sometimes wreak havoc during childhood and later are related, at least in their quasi-neurotic form, to these ambivalences more than to the mere influence of the orders and of the initial respect.[28]

3. *Moral Realism*

From the standpoint of moral judgment, heteronomy leads to a systematic structure that is preoperatory both with reference to the relational cognitive mechanisms and to the processes of socialization. This structure is *moral realism,* according to which obligations and values are determined by the law or the order itself, independent of intentions and relationships.

One of us observed a young child who was habitually

[28] Guilt begets feelings of anxiety, which have been studied, notably by Charles Odier (*L'Angoisse et la pensée magique,* Neuchâtel: Delachaux et Niestlé, 1947) and by Anna Freud (*The Ego and the Mechanisms of Defense,* rev. ed., New York: International Universities Press, 1967), along with the defense mechanisms that these anxieties provoke. The child feels guilty for having been hostile, and the anxiety born of this guilt leads to self-punishments, sacrifices, etc., and is sometimes combined, as Odier has shown, with certain quasi-magical forms of precausality (see above, pages 110 ff.) as instruments of defense and protection. (Indeed, these mechanisms are not limited to moral anxieties: a young boy who was later to become a mathematician took a different route on his second visit to the dentist because the first visit had hurt—as if the pain depended on the route he took to get there.)

subjected to a maternal order of no moral importance (to finish a certain part of the meal). When one day this order was waived by the mother herself because the child was indisposed, the child could not help feeling bound by the order and guilty for not respecting it.

Moral realism leads to *objective responsibility*, whereby an act is evaluated in terms of the degree to which it conforms to the law rather than with reference to whether there is malicious intent to violate the law or whether the intent is good but in involuntary conflict with the law.[29] The child, for example, is told not to lie long before he understands the social value of this order (for lack of sufficient socialization), and sometimes before he is able to distinguish intentional deception from the distortions of reality that are due to symbolic play or to simple desire. As a result, veracity is external to the personality of the subject and gives rise to moral realism and objective responsibility whereby a lie appears to be serious not to the degree that it corresponds to the intent to deceive, but to the degree that it differs materially from the objective truth. One of us set up the comparison of a real lie (telling your family you got a good mark in school when you weren't called on to recite) to a simple exaggeration (telling, after being frightened by a dog, that he was as big as a horse or a cow). For young children, the first lie is not "naughty," because (1) it often happens that one gets good marks; and above all (2) "Mama believed it!" The second "lie," however, is very naughty, because nobody ever saw a dog *that* size.

[29] In primitive law, homicide is criminal even if it is accidental and not the result of negligence. Touching the ark of the covenant is a violation of a taboo, even in case of immediate danger.

4. *Autonomy*

With advances in social cooperation and the corresponding operatory progress, the child arrives at new moral relationships based on *mutual respect* which lead to a certain *autonomy*. One must not, of course, exaggerate the importance of these factors in relation to the preceding ones. However, two important facts should be noted:

First, in games with rules, children before the age of seven who receive the rules ready-made from their elders (by a mechanism derived from unilateral respect) regard them as "sacred," untouchable, and of transcendent origin (parents, the government, God, etc.). Older children, on the contrary, regard rules as the result of agreement among contemporaries, and accept the idea that rules can be changed by means of a democratically arrived at consensus.

Second, an essential product of mutual respect and reciprocity is the sense of justice, which is often acquired at the expense of the parents (on the occasion of an involuntary injustice, for example). As early as seven or eight and increasingly thereafter, justice prevails over obedience itself and becomes a central norm, equivalent in the affective realm to the norms of coherence in the realm of the cognitive operations. (Indeed, on the level of cooperation and mutual respect there is a striking parallelism between these operations and the structuration of moral values.[30]

---

[30] Finally, let us note that by studying sociometric choices in groups of children in the sense of J. L. Moreno but without reference to his rather audacious theories, B. Reymond-Rivier (*Choix sociométriques et motivations*, Neuchâtel: Delachaux et

VI. *Conclusion*

What is most striking about this long period of preparation for and formation of the concrete operations is the functional unity (within each subperiod) that binds cognitive, playful, affective, social, and moral reactions into a whole. Indeed, if we compare the preoperatory subperiod between two and seven or eight with the subperiod of completion between seven or eight and eleven or twelve, we see the unfolding of a long, integrated process that may be characterized as a transition from subjective centering in all areas to a decentering that is at once cognitive, social, and moral. This process is all the more remarkable in that it reproduces and develops on a large scale at the level of thought what has already taken place on a small scale at the sensori-motor level (Chapter 1, pages 13 ff. and 21 ff.).

Representative intelligence begins with the child's systematic concentration on his own action and on the momentary figurative aspects of the segments of reality with which this action deals. Later it arrives at a decentering based on the general coordination of action, and this permits the formation of operatory systems of transformations and constants or conservations which liberate the representation of reality from its deceptive figurative appearances.

Niestlé, 1961), succeeded in showing a clear-cut development in the reasons invoked for choosing "leaders." Whereas small children give reasons that are partially heteronomous (approval of teachers, standing in school, etc.), older children invoke criteria that clearly belong to the second group of values: fairness, not being a tattletale, knowing how to keep a secret (among girls), etc.

Play, a zone of interference between cognitive and affective interests, makes its appearance during the subperiod between two and seven or eight with the apogee of symbolic play, which is an assimilation of reality to the self and its desires, and later evolves in the direction of games of construction and games with rules, which mark an objectivization of the symbol and a socialization of the self.

Affectivity, initially centered on familial complexes, gradually widens its scope in proportion to the expansion of social relations, and the moral feelings initially dependent on an external sacred authority, which succeeds in evoking only a relative obedience, evolve in the direction of a mutual respect and reciprocity whose decentering effects are, in our societies, much more profound and permanent.

Finally, social exchanges, which include all the preceding reactions, since they are both personal and interpersonal at the same time, give rise to a process of gradual structuration or socialization which leads from a state of relative lack of coordination or differentiation between the child's own point of view and that of others to a state of coordination of points of view and cooperation in action and communication. This process includes all the others. A child of four or five, for example, is often not aware that he is himself the brother or sister of his brother or sister. This lack of perspective affects the logic of relations as well as the awareness of self. When he reaches the level of operations, he will by that very fact be capable of cooperation—and it is impossible to separate cause from effect in this integrated process.

5

THE PREADOLESCENT
AND THE PROPOSITIONAL
OPERATIONS

THE SAME UNITY of behavior encountered earlier in the
various stages is found again between eleven or twelve
and fourteen or fifteen, when the subject succeeds in free-
ing himself from the concrete and in locating reality
within a group of possible transformations. This final fundamental decentering, which occurs at the end of childhood, prepares for adolescence, whose principal characteristic is a similar liberation from the concrete in favor of
interest oriented toward the non-present and the future.
This is the age of great ideals and of the beginning of
theories, as well as the time of simple present adaptation
to reality. This affective and social impulse of adolescence has often been described. But it has not always
been understood that this impulse is dependent upon a

transformation of thought that permits the handling of hypotheses and reasoning with regard to propositions removed from concrete and present observation.

This new structure of thought is formed during preadolescence, and it is important to describe and analyze it as a structure, something which the devisers of "tests" too often forget, overlooking the common and general characteristics in favor of individual differences. There is only one way to get at the structures as such, and that is by isolating their logical aspects. This does not mean falling prey to logicism, but simply using a general and qualitative algebra instead of (or before) resorting to statistical qualification. The particular advantage of this algebra is that it provides a table of the potentialities that a normal subject may utilize—though, of course, every subject does not realize all of them. Moreover, their realization is subject to accelerations or retardations, according to the scholastic or social milieu.

The study of these preadolescent substructures is particularly important to an integrated picture of child psychology, for they constitute a natural culmination of the sensori-motor structures (Chapter 1) and of the groupings of concrete operations (Chapter 4). Although in a sense these new transformations mark the end of childhood, they are no less essential to this discussion. They not only open up new perspectives into later stages of psychological development, but they also represent a completion of the preceding stages. Indeed, it is not a question of adding another story to an edifice to which it bears no relation; rather, we have here a group of syntheses or structurations which, although new, are a direct and natural extension of the preceding ones and fill in some of the gaps left by them.

I. *Formal Thought and the Combinatorial System*

The concrete operations relate directly to objects and to groups of objects (classes), to the relations between objects and to the counting of objects. Thus, the logical organization of judgments and arguments is inseparable from their content. That is, the operations function only with reference to observations or representations regarded as true, and not on the basis of mere hypotheses. The great novelty of this stage is that by means of a differentiation of form and content the subject becomes capable of reasoning correctly about propositions he does not believe, or at least not yet; that is, propositions that he considers pure hypotheses. He becomes capable of drawing the necessary conclusions from truths which are merely possible, which constitutes the beginning of hypothetico-deductive or formal thought.

1. *The Combinatorial System*

The first result of this "disconnection" of thought from objects is to liberate relations and classifications from their concrete or intuitive ties. Up to now both were bound by the essentially concrete condition of a step-by-step progression based on graduated resemblances; and even in a zoological classification (for these remain on the level of the "grouping") you cannot extract two non-contiguous classes, like oysters and camels, and make them into a new "natural" class. With the liberation of form from content, however, it becomes possible to establish any relations or classes that are desired by bringing together any elements singly, in twos, threes, etc. This generalization of the operations of classification and of relations of order culminates in a *combinatorial system* (combinations, permutations, etc.), the simplest of which consists in the actual combinatorial operations, or classification of all classifications.

This combinatorial system is of prime importance in the extension and reinforcement of the powers of thought. Once established, it enables the subject to combine among themselves objects with objects or factors with factors (physical, etc.), or similarly ideas or propositions (which gives rise to a new logic), and, consequently, to reason about a given reality (a segment of physical reality, an explanation based on factors, or a theory in the simple sense of a group of related propositions) by considering this reality no longer in its limited and concrete aspects but in terms of some or all of the possible combinations. This considerably reinforces the deductive powers of intelligence.

2. Combinations of Objects

One can ask the child, for example, to combine colored counters in twos, threes, etc., or to subject them to permutations according to the various possible orders. At the level of the concrete operations, these combinations always remain incomplete, because the subject adopts a step-by-step method, without generalizing. At the preadolescent level, however, the child manages easily (after the age of twelve for combinations, a little later for permutations) to find an exhaustive method—without, of course, discovering the formula (which he is not asked to do), but by working out a system that takes account of all possibilities.[1]

3. Propositional Combinations

The combination of factors will be discussed later on. In speaking of the combination of ideas or propositions, one must refer to modern symbolic or algorithmic logic, which is much closer to the real working of thought than the syllogistic logic of Aristotle.[2]

[1] Similarly, as described in Bärbel Inhelder and Jean Piaget, *The Growth of Logical Thinking from Childhood to Adolescence* (New York: Basic Books, 1958), you present the child with five jars A through E containing colorless liquids. The combination of A, C, and E produces a yellow color; B is a bleaching agent and D is pure water. The child has seen the color but not the method of obtaining it. The problem presented to him (with G. Noelting) is to discover the combination that will produce the color and to determine the roles of B and D. At age seven to eleven the child generally proceeds by combinations of two's and then jumps to a trial of all five together. After the age of twelve he proceeds methodically, testing all possible combinations of one, two, three, four, and five elements, and thus solves the problem.

[2] Let p be a proposition, $\bar{p}$ its negative, q another proposition and $\bar{q}$ its negative. You can group them multiplicatively, which gives $p \cdot q$ (this animal is a swan and is white), $\bar{p} \cdot q$ (it is not a swan, but it is white), $p \cdot \bar{q}$ (it is white, but not a swan), or $\bar{p} \cdot \bar{q}$ (it is neither a swan nor white). This is not a combinatorial system but a simple multiplicative "grouping" that a child is capable of after the age of seven or eight (Chapter 4, page 103). From these four multiplicative associations, however, sixteen combinations may be derived by taking them one at a time, two at a time, three at a time, or four at a time, or by taking none. Using the sign ($\cdot$) to express conjunction and the sign (v) disjunction, we have, in fact: (1) $p \cdot q$; (2) $p \cdot \bar{q}$; (3) $\bar{p} \cdot q$; (4) $\bar{p} \cdot \bar{q}$; (5) $p \cdot q \vee \bar{p} \cdot \bar{q}$;

The child of twelve to fifteen of course does not establish the relevant laws of logic, nor will he write down the formula for the number of all possible combinations of the colored counters. But it is remarkable that at the level at which he becomes capable of combining elements by an

---

(6) $p \cdot \bar{q} \vee \bar{p} \cdot q$; (7) $p \cdot q \vee p \cdot \bar{q}$; (8) $p \cdot q \vee \bar{p} \cdot q$; etc.—or four associations with one term, six with two terms, four with three terms, one with four terms, and one with no terms. These sixteen combinations (or 256 combinations in the case of three propositions, etc.) constitute new and altogether distinct operations which may be called "propositional," since they consist in combining propositions from the point of view only of their being true or false. For example, if the four associations indicated are true, then there is no relation necessarily between swans and whiteness. Before the discovery of the black swans of Australia, however, we would have said that the association $p \cdot \bar{q}$ was false. That would have left "$p \cdot q$ or $\bar{p} \cdot q$ or $\bar{p} \cdot \bar{q}$"; that is, an implication: swan implies whiteness, because if it is a swan it is white; but an object may be white without being a swan ($\bar{p} \cdot q$) or be neither white nor a swan ($\bar{p} \cdot \bar{q}$).

These propositional operations are not simply a new way of expressing the facts. On the contrary, they constitute true logic, which is much richer than the "logic" of the concrete operations. In the first place, they are necessary for formal reasoning on hypotheses stated verbally, as in a discussion or a coherent presentation. In the second place, they may be applied to experimental and physical data, as we shall see in Sections III and IV below, and they are necessary for a dissociation of factors (combinatorial system) and therefore the exclusion of false hypotheses (Section IV) and the construction of complex explanatory schemes (Section III). In the third place, they constitute an extension and generalization of the concrete operations, which are incomplete in themselves, for a combinatorial system is a classification of classifications, and the group of the two reversibilities (Section II) is the synthesis of all groupings. The propositional operations, then, represent operations to the second power, but with reference to concrete operations (since every proposition represents, in its content, the result of a concrete operation).

exhaustive and systematic method he is also capable of combining ideas or hypotheses in affirmative or negative statements, and thus of utilizing propositional operations hitherto unknown to him: implication (if—then), disjunction (either—or, or both), exclusion (either—or) or incompatibility (either—or, or neither—neither), reciprocal implication, etc.

II. *The Two Reversibilities*

At the formal level, the liberation of thought mechanisms from content results in the formation of a combinatorial system and also in the elaboration of a fundamental structure that marks both the synthesis of the previous "groupings" and the starting point for a series of new advances.

The groupings of concrete operations which we reviewed in outline in Chapter 4, pages 96 ff., are of two kinds and exhibit two fundamental forms of reversibility that, at the age of seven to eleven, are the culmination of a process going back to the sensori-motor schemes and the preoperatory representative regulations.

The first of these forms of reversibility is *inversion* or negation; its characteristic is that the inverse operation combined with the corresponding direct operation cancels the whole thing out: $+ A - A = 0$. Negation has its origins in the most primitive forms of behavior: a baby can put an object in front of himself, then push it away; when he starts to talk, he is able to say "no" before he says "yes." At the level of the first preoperatory classifications he is able to add an object to others, or take it away. The generalization and particularly the exact structuration of such behavior patterns of inversion characterize the first operations and their strict reversibility. In this respect, inversion characterizes class groupings, whether additive (the elimination of an object or group of objects) or multiplicative (the inverse of the multiplication of two classes is the "abstraction" or elimination of an intersection).[3]

The second form of reversibility is *reciprocity* or symmetry. Its characteristic is that the original operation combined with its reciprocal results in an equivalence. If, for example, the original operation consists in introducing a difference between A and B in the form of $A < B$, and the reciprocal operation consists in canceling out this difference or expressing it the other way around, you end up with the equivalence $A = A$ (or if $A \leqslant B$ and $B \geqslant A$, then $A = B$). Reciprocity is the form of reversibility which characterizes relational groupings, but it also has its source in early behavior patterns of a symmetrical nature. There are spatial symmetries, perceptive symmetries, representative symmetries, motor symmetries, etc. At the level of the preoperatory representative regulations, a child will say that when a ball of dough is rolled into a sausage it contains more dough because it is longer. If you keep making the sausage longer, however, he will change his opinion, by regulatory and not operatory reciprocity, and he will say that the sausage contains less dough because it is so thin. Both kinds of reversibility exist at the level of concrete operations. Lengthening can be negated by shortening or compensated for by thinning.

[3] For example, white crows, apart from their whiteness, are still crows.

At the level of the groupings of concrete operations, each of the two forms of reversibility rules its separate domain, the system of classes or that of relations. The child does not yet have at his disposal an integrated system that would enable him to pass deductively from one set of groupings to another and to compose thereby the inverse and reciprocal transformations. The concrete operations, whatever their advances over the preoperatory regulations, remain incomplete, and the combinatorial system makes it possible to fill in one of the gaps.

The combination of inversions and reciprocities into a single system is attended by a process analogous to and inseparable from that which occurs in the constitution of the combinatorial system.

The liberation of the formal mechanisms from content leads the child to free himself from the step-by-step groupings and to try to combine inversions and reciprocities. The combinatorial system leads him to superimpose on the elementary operations a new system of operations on operations, or propositional operations (whose content consists of operations of class, of relation, or of number, whereas their form constitutes a combinatorial system that includes them all). The new operations, being combinatory, include all the combinations—inversions and reciprocities as well.

The new system which now emerges clearly involves synthesis or completion, though it too will be integrated into a larger system. There is not merely a juxtaposition of inversions and reciprocities, but an operatory fusion into a whole. Henceforth every operation will at once be the inverse of another and the reciprocal of a third, which gives four transformations: direct, inverse, reciprocal, and inverse of the reciprocal, the latter also being the correlative (or dual) of the first.

Let us take as an example the implication $p \supset q$, and let us imagine an experimental situation in which a child between twelve and fifteen tries to understand the connections between phenomena which are not familiar to him but which he analyzes by means of the new propositional operations rather than by trial and error. Let us suppose then that he observes a moving object that keeps starting and stopping and he notices that the stops seem to be accompanied by the lighting of an electric bulb. The first hypothesis he will make is that the light is the cause (or an indication of the cause) of the stops, or $p \supset q$ (light implies stop). There is only one way to confirm the hypothesis, and that is to find out whether the bulb ever lights up without the object stopping, or $p \cdot \bar{q}$ ($p \cdot \bar{q}$ is the inverse or negation of $p \supset q$). But he may also wonder whether the light, instead of causing the stop, is caused by it, or $q \supset p$ (now the reciprocal and not the inverse of $p \supset q$). To confirm $q \supset p$ (stop implies light), he looks for the opposite case which would disconfirm it; that is, does the object ever stop without the light going on? This case, $\bar{p} \cdot q$, is the inverse of $q \supset p$. It is at the same time a correlative of $p \supset q$. The object stopping every time the light goes on is quite compatible with its sometimes stopping for some other reason. Similarly, $p \cdot \bar{q}$, which is the inverse of $p \supset q$, is also the correlative of $q \supset p$. If every time there is a stop the bulb lights up ($q \supset p$), there can be lights without stops. Similarly, if $q \supset p$ is the reciprocal of $p \supset q$, then $\bar{p} \cdot q$ is also the reciprocal of $p \cdot \bar{q}$.

Thus, without knowing any logical formula, or the formal criteria for a mathematical "group" (any more than the baby knows this definition when he discovers the sensori-motor group of displacements), the preadolescent of twelve to fifteen is capable of manipulating transformations according to the four possibilities; I (identical transformation), N (inverse transformation), R (reciprocal transformation), and C (correlative transformation). In the case of $p \supset q$ these four operations are:

$$I = p \supset q; N = p \cdot \bar{q}; R = q \supset p; \text{ and } C = \bar{p} \cdot q.$$

But $N = RC$, $R = NC$, $C = NR$, and $I = NRC$,[4] which constitutes a group of four transformations, labeled the 4-group, combining inversions and reciprocities into a single system, and thus achieving a synthesis of the hitherto partial structures.

III. *The Formal Operatory Schemes*

At eleven or twelve a series of new operatory schemes is established whose nearly simultaneous appearance seems to indicate a connection between them but whose structural affinity, stemming from the 4-group, is difficult to see when looking at these schemes from the subject's point of view. These schemes are the notions of proportion, the double systems of reference, the comprehension of a hydrostatic equilibrium, certain forms of probability, etc.

On analysis, each of these schemes is found to involve either a combinatorial system (but rarely only that) or a

---

[4] This means that $N = (p \cdot \bar{q})$ is the reciprocal R of $C = (\bar{p} \cdot q)$; that $R = (q \cdot p)$ is the inverse N of the correlative $(\bar{p} \cdot q)$; etc.

system of four transformations belonging to the 4-group just mentioned—which indicates how general the group is, although the subject, of course, is not aware of its existence as such.

1. *Proportions*

The relation between the 4-group and numerical or metrical proportion is clear. (The value of a function can be modified in the same direction either by adding to the numerator or subtracting from the denominator.) What is less clear before studies were made on the development of logic in the child is, first, that the 4-group is an interpropositional structure, and, second, that the notion of proportion emerges in a qualitative and logical form before being structured quantitatively.

The notion of proportion appears at eleven or twelve in several different areas and always in the same initially qualitative form. These areas are, among others, spatial proportions (similar figures), metrical speeds ($S/T = NS/NT$), probabilities ($x/y = nx/ny$), relations between weights and lengths of the arms of a balance, etc.

Concerning the balance, for example, the subject first by ordinal reasoning discovers that the greater the weight, the lower the arm and the farther from the line of equilibrium. This leads him to discover a linear function and to understand a first condition of equilibrium (the equality of weights at equal distances from the central pivot). Also by ordinal reasoning, he discovers that a single weight W pulls the arm down more the farther it is placed from the pivot. From this he also derives a linear function and understands that equilibrium is attained for two equal weights provided they are equidistant from the pivot, however long the distance L may be. The discovery of the inverse proportionality between W and L is also obtained by a qualitative coordination of these two initially ordinal functions. Comprehension begins when the child discovers that the result stays the same if he increases a weight without changing the distance from the center on the one side, while increasing the distance without changing the weight on the other. From this he derives the hypothesis (which he verifies in an ordinal manner) that when you begin with two equal weights at equal distances from the center, you maintain equilibrium by decreasing one weight but moving it farther away or by increasing the other weight and moving it closer to the center. It is only then that he grasps the simple metrical proportion $\dfrac{W}{L} = \dfrac{2W}{2L}$, etc., but he discovers this by beginning with the qualitative proportion; that is, that decreasing the weight and increasing the length is equivalent to increasing the weight and decreasing the length.[5]

[5] The scheme of proportionality is derived directly from the 4-group. The subject begins with two transformations, each of which involves an inverse: increasing (or decreasing) the weight or the length ($+W$ and $+L$). Then he discovers that the inverse of one (decrease of weight, or $-W$) may be replaced by the inverse of the other (decrease of length, or $-L$), which is not identical to the first inverse but leads to the same result by compensation and not by cancellation. If $+W$ is regarded as the basic operation (I) and $-W$ as the inverse (N), then $-L$ is the reciprocal (R) of $+W$ and $+L$ is its correlative (C). Since two pairs of direct and inverse transformations are involved, along with a relation of equivalence (but not of identity), the system of proportion must derive from the 4-group and takes the form $I/R = C/N$ (or by crossed products $IN = RC$).

2. *Double Systems of Reference*

The same is true of double systems of reference. A snail moves along a board in one direction or the other, and the board itself advances or retreats in relation to an external point of reference. The child at the level of concrete operations understands these two pairs of direct and inverse operations but does not succeed in combining them and fails to anticipate, for example, that the snail, even as he moves forward, may remain motionless in relation to the external surroundings, if the movement of the board compensates for that of the animal's. As soon as the 4-group is acquired, however, the solution is made easy by the introduction of compensation without cancellation; that is, reciprocity (R). In this case we have $I \cdot R = N \cdot C$, in which (I) is the movement of the snail to the right; (R) the movement of the board to the left; (N) the movement of the snail to the left; and (C) the movement of the board to the right.

3. *Hydrostatic Equilibrium*

In a U tube a piston whose weight can be increased or decreased is placed in one arm, so that the level of the liquid in the other arm can be changed; the specific weight of the liquid (alcohol, water, or glycerin) can also be varied. The problem here is to understand that the weight of the liquid acts in the opposite direction to the weight of the piston, as a reaction opposed to its action. It is interesting to note that until about nine or ten this reaction or resistance of the liquid is not understood as such. The child thinks the weight of the liquid is added to that of the piston and acts in the same direction. Here again, the mechanism can be understood only in terms of the 4-group: if (I) = the increase of the weight of the piston and (N) = its decrease, then the increase of the specific weight of the liquid is a reciprocal (R) in relation to (I) and its decrease a correlative (C).

4. *Notions of Probability*

A fundamental group of operatory schemes also made accessible by formal operations relates to probability and results from an assimilation of the concept of chance by means of these operations. In order to estimate, for example, the probability that two or three balls of the same color will be drawn at random from a bag containing fifteen red balls, ten blue balls, eight green balls, etc., the child must be capable of at least two operations characteristic of this level. He must be able to apply a combinatorial system that enables him to take into consideration all the possible combinations of the given elements; and he must be able to calculate proportions, however elementary, so that he can grasp the fact (which eludes subjects on the previous levels) that probabilities like 3/9 and 2/6, etc., are equivalent. It is not until the age of eleven or twelve that the child understands combinatorial probabilities or such notions as fluctuation, correlation, or even probable compensations with the increase of numbers. It is particularly striking to observe how late the "law of large numbers" is grasped: young subjects are willing to anticipate a uniformity of distributions only up to a certain limit (what might be called "small large numbers").

IV. *The Induction of Laws and the Dissociation of Factors*

The propositional operations are naturally much more closely related than the "concrete" operations to a precise and flexible manipulation of language, for in order to manipulate propositions and hypotheses, one must be able to combine them verbally. It would be erroneous to imagine, however, that the only intellectual advances of the preadolescent and the adolescent are those marked by improvement in language. The examples mentioned in the preceding paragraphs indicate that the combinatorial system and double reversibility affect the conquest of reality as well as the capacity for clear formulation.

There is one remarkable aspect of thought at this stage which was largely overlooked because traditional instruction in schools almost totally ignored it (in defiance of the most obvious technical and scientific requirements of modern society), namely, the spontaneous development of an experimental spirit, which is impossible to establish at the level of concrete operations but which the combinatorial system and the propositional structures render accessible, once the proper occasion is provided. Here are three examples:

1. *Elasticity*

One of the authors presented subjects with mechanisms, the problem being to discover the laws that governed their functioning. The situations presented involved several factors, among which the child had to choose those that were effective. Once he had made this more or less complex induction, he was asked to furnish detailed proof of his conclusions—in particular, proof of the effective or non-effective role played by each of the factors spontaneously enumerated. Thus, by observing successively the inductive process and the method of verification, the experimenter is in a position to judge whether the subject has arrived at an adequate experimental method involving dissociation of factors and respective variation of each of them while neutralizing the others.

For example, the subject is presented with a number of metal rods which he can fasten at one end, the problem being to account for their differences in flexibility. The factors involved in this experiment are the length of the rods, their thickness, their cross section, and the material they are made of (in our experiment, steel and brass, whose moduli of elasticity are quite different). At the level of concrete operations, the subject does not attempt to make a preliminary inventory of the factors but proceeds directly to action by means of seriation and serial correspondence: examining longer and longer rods and seeing whether they are increasingly flexible, etc. In case of interference between two factors, the second is analyzed in turn by the same method, but without systematic dissociation.

When asked to furnish proof, subjects of nine or ten will choose a long thin rod and a short thick one to demonstrate the role of length, because in this way, as a boy of nine and a half told us, "you can see the difference better"! From eleven or twelve onward (with a leveling off at fourteen to fifteen), subjects, after a little groping, make a list of factors by way of hypothesis, and then study them one by one. The advance over the earlier performance is shown by the fact that they dissociate each from the others. That is, they vary each factor alone, keeping all the other factors constant. For example, they choose two rods of the same width, the same cross section (square, rectangular, or cylindrical), and the same substance, varying only the length. This method, which becomes fairly general at about fourteen, is all the more remarkable in that none of the subjects we interviewed had received instruction in this method in school.

It is not taught in school (and if it were, it would still have to be assimilated by the necessary logical structures), and must be the direct result of propositional operations. On the one hand, the dissociation of factors presupposes a combinatorial system; that is, the variation of one factor at a time (which is sufficient in the experiment in question, where all factors act positively), two at a time, etc. On the other hand, in a complex system of influences, the concrete operations of classification, seriation, correspondence, measurement, etc., are not sufficient, and it is necessary to introduce implications, disjunctions, exclusions, etc., which belong to the propositional operations and which presuppose both a combinatorial system and coordinations of inversion and reciprocity (4-group system).

2. *The Pendulum*

A second example will help to explain the logical complexity which is inevitably introduced whenever there is concurrence of *real* and *apparent* factors. (It is not for nothing that experimental physics has always been centuries behind mathematics and logic.) The pendulum in the experiment can be made to swing faster or slower by

F

varying the length of the string, the rate of oscillation remaining unaffected by differences in the attached weight,
the height from which the weight is dropped, or the initial
impetus. Subjects at the level of concrete operations vary
everything at the same time and are convinced that varying the weight has an effect (most adults start with the
same idea). The children have great difficulty in exclud-
ing the weight factor, for when they simultaneously vary
the length of the cord and the weight, they generally find
"good" reasons to justify the influence of weight. The preadolescent, however, by dissociating the factors, observes
that the weight can vary without altering the frequency of
oscillation and vice versa, so he excludes the weight factor; and the same is true of the height of the fall and the
initial impetus which the subject can impart to the weight.[6]

[6] *Conservation of movement.* There is no need to provide ad-
ditional data on this, but it may be of interest to point out that, in a
certain sense, the beginnings of experimental induction lead to
reasonings analogous to the beginnings of Galilean physics.
Aristotle conceived of induction as an amplifying generalization, a
conception which did not allow him to carry his physics as far as
his logic. (With respect to the notion of speed, he does not go
beyond purely concrete operations.) The empiricists proceeded
along the same lines. They saw induction as a recording of the data
of experience, without understanding the fundamental role of
structuration of reality played by the logico-mathematical operations, notably by the formal structures under discussion. This structuration immediately enables some subjects (we do not say all,
but we have observed many) to begin to understand a form of conservation that is impossible to observe in its pure state; that is, the
principle of inertia—a model of deductive and theoretical interpretation. In analyzing the movements of marbles of different
weight and volume over a horizontal plane, these subjects observe
that the marbles come to rest as a function of the resistance of the
air, of friction, etc. If p stands for immobility and q, r, s . . .
stand for the factors at work (v is the symbol of disjunction), we

V. *The Affective Transformations*

It has long been thought that the affective changes characteristic of adolescence, beginning between the ages of twelve and fifteen, are to be explained primarily by innate and quasi-instinctive mechanisms. This is assumed by psychoanalysts who base their interpretations of these stages of development on the hypothesis of a "new version of the Oedipus complex." In reality, the role of social factors (in the twofold sense of socialization and cultural transmission) is far more important and is favored more than was suspected by the intellectual transformations we have been discussing.

Indeed, the essential difference between formal thought and concrete operations is that the latter are centered on reality, whereas the former grasps the possible transformations and assimilates reality only in terms of imagined or deduced events. The change of perspective is as important for affective as for cognitive development, for the world of values also can remain bound by concrete and perceptible reality, or it can encompass many interpersonal and social possibilities.

Adolescence (fifteen to eighteen) is the age of the individual's introduction into adult society much more than it is the age of puberty. Preadolescence is characterized both by an acceleration of physiological and somatic

---

have: $(p) \supset (q \vee r \vee s \ldots)$. From this they conclude that by eliminating these factors they would eliminate the stops: $(\bar{q} \cdot \bar{r} \cdot \bar{s} \ldots) \supset \bar{p}$. Thus we have the beginning of an intuition of inertial movement, directly derived from the reversibility of the nascent propositional operations.

growth and by the opening up of new possibilities for which the subject is preparing himself, for he can anticipate them by means of the deductive capabilities he has acquired.

Each new mental structure, by integrating the preceding ones, succeeds both in partly liberating the individual from his past and in inaugurating new activities which at the formal operatory level are mainly oriented toward the future. Yet clinical psychology, and especially the kind of psychoanalysis currently in vogue, often sees nothing in affectivity but a series of repetitions or analogies with the past (new versions of the Oedipus complex, narcissism, etc.). It is true that Anna Freud [7] and E. Erikson[8] stressed "successive identifications" with elders who serve as models, thus liberating children from infantile choices (with the concomitant danger of identity diffusion according to Erikson), but they have neglected the role of the "concrete autonomy" acquired during later childhood (Chapter 4, page 127) and above all the role of cognitive constructions that pave the way for an anticipation of the future and a receptiveness to new values.

The moral autonomy which emerges on the interpersonal level between the ages of seven and twelve acquires, with formal thought, an added dimension in the application of ideal or supra-individual values. One of us, who once studied with A. M. Weil [9] the development of the

[7] Anna Freud, *The Ego and the Mechanisms of Defense* (rev. ed., New York: International Universities Press, 1967).

[8] E. Erikson, *Childhood and Society* (2nd ed.; New York: W. W. Norton, 1963).

[9] Jean Piaget and A. M. Weil, "Le Développement chez l'enfant de l'idée de patrie et des relations avec l'étranger," *Bulletin international des sciences sociales UNESCO,* III (1951), 605–621.

concept "native land," observed that this concept did not acquire adequate affective value until the age of twelve or over. The same is true of the concept of social justice and of rational, aesthetic, or social ideals. As a result of the acquisition of such values, decisions, whether in opposition to or in agreement with the adult, have an altogether different significance than they do in the small social groups of younger children. This is particularly true within the high-school community. The possibilities opened up by these new values are obvious in the adolescent, who differs from the child in that he is not only capable of forming theories but is also concerned with choosing a career that will permit him to satisfy his need for social reform and for new ideas. The preadolescent has not yet reached this stage, but there are many indications, in this transitional phase, of the beginnings of the creation of ideas and the formation of values related to plans for the future. Unfortunately, few studies have been made that are directly relevant to this subject.[10]

[10] One reason among others is the extent to which well-known studies on adolescence (G. Stanley Hall, O. Spranger, Charlotte Bühler, M. Debesse, and others) are bound up with our society and even with certain social classes, so that the question arises whether the "crises" so often described do not amount to a kind of social artifact. Margaret Mead in Samoa, and B. Malinowski among the Trobrianders of New Guinea, did not find the same affective manifestations, and Schelsky, in his investigation of *Die skeptische Generation*, shows how these manifestations vary within our own society. Certainly an essential sociological factor is the attitude of adult society toward the adolescent and preadolescent. Negligible in conservative societies, the adolescent is the man of tomorrow in countries in the throes of change. Obviously such factors, along with family attitudes, play an essential role in this complex development.

Conclusion

FACTORS IN
MENTAL DEVELOPMENT

BASICALLY, the mental development of the child appears as a succession of three great periods. Each of these extends the preceding period, reconstructs it on a new level, and later surpasses it to an ever greater degree. This is true even of the first period, for the evolution of the sensori-motor schemes extends and surpasses the evolution of the organic structures which takes place during embryogenesis. Semiotic relations, thought, and interpersonal connections internalize these schemes of action by reconstructing them on the new level of representation, and surpass them until all the concrete operations and cooperative structures have been established. Finally, after the age of eleven or twelve, nascent formal thought restructures the concrete operations by subordinating them to new structures whose development will continue throughout adolescence and all of later life (along with many other trans-formations as well).

The integration of successive structures, each of which leads to the emergence of the subsequent one, makes it possible to divide the child's development into long periods or stages and subperiods or substages which can be characterized as follows: (1) Their order of succession is constant, although the average ages at which they occur may vary with the individual, according to his degree of intelligence or with the social milieu. Thus the unfolding of the stages may give rise to accelerations or retardations, but their sequence remains constant in the areas (operations, etc.) in which such stages have been shown to exist. (2) Each stage is characterized by an overall structure in terms of which the main behavior patterns can be explained. In order to establish such explanatory stages it is not sufficient to refer to these patterns as such or to the predominance of a given characteristic (as is the case with the stages proposed by Freud and Wallon). (3) These overall structures are integrative and non-interchangeable. Each results from the preceding one, integrating it as a subordinate structure, and prepares for the subsequent one, into which it is sooner or later itself integrated.

Given the existence of such a development and the integrative direction that can be seen in it *a posteriori,* the problem is to understand its mechanism. This is, in fact, an extension of the problem embryologists raise when they wonder whether ontogenetic organization results from pre-formation or from epigenesis, and what causal processes are involved. As yet we have reached only provisional solutions, and future theories will be acceptable only if they succeed in integrating interpretations of embryogenesis, organic growth, and mental development into a harmonious whole. Meanwhile, we must be content with a discussion of the four general factors so far assigned to mental development:

1. The first of these is organic growth and especially the maturation of the nervous system and the endocrine systems. There is no doubt that a number of behavior patterns depend on the first functionings of certain structures or circuits. This is true of the coordination of vision and prehension at about four and a half months. The organic conditions for visual perception are not fully realized until adolescence, whereas retinal functioning is quite early (Chapter 2, page 29 n.).

Maturation plays a role throughout mental growth. But what role? We have little detailed knowledge about maturation, and we know next to nothing about the conditions that permit the formation of the general operatory structures. Where we do have some data, we see that maturation consists essentially of opening up new possibilities and thus constitutes a necessary but not in itself a sufficient condition for the appearance of certain behavior patterns. The possibilities thus opened up also need to be fulfilled, and for this to occur, the maturation must be reinforced by functional exercise and a *minimum* of experience. In addition, the further the acquisitions are removed from their sensori-motor origins, the more variable is their chronology, meaning not their sequence but the time of appearance. Maturation is only one of many factors involved and the influence of the physical and social milieu increases in importance with the child's growth.

Organic maturation is undoubtedly a necessary factor and plays an indispensable role in the unvarying order of succession of the stages of the child's development, but it does not explain all development and represents only one factor among several.

2. A second fundamental factor is the role of exercise and of acquired experience in the actions performed upon objects (as opposed to social experience). This is also an essential and necessary factor, even in the formation of the logico-mathematical structures. But it does not by itself explain everything, despite the claims of empiricists. It is highly complex, because there are two types of experience: (a) physical experience, which consists of acting upon objects in order to abstract their properties (for example, comparing two weights independently of volume); and (b) logico-mathematical experience, which consists of acting upon objects with a view to learning the result of the coordination of the actions (for example, when a child of five or six discovers empirically that the sum of a group of objects is independent of their spatial disposition or the order in which they are counted). In (b), knowledge is derived from action (which organizes or combines) rather than from the objects; experience in this case is simply the practical and quasi-motor phase of what will later be operatory deduction, which is not to be equated with experience in the sense of action of the external milieu; on the contrary, it is a question of constructive action performed by the subject upon external objects. As for (a), physical experience is by no means a simple recording of phenomena but constitutes an active structuration, since it always involves an *assimilation* to logico-mathematical structures (thus, comparing two weights presupposes the establishment of a relation, and therefore the construction of a logical form). The preceding chapters of this book

F*

show that the elaboration of the logico-mathematical structures (from the sensori-motor level to formal thought) precedes physical knowledge. The permanent object (Chapter 1, pages 14 ff.) is inseparable from the group of displacements, just as the variation of physical factors (Chapter 5, pages 145 ff.) is part of a combinatorial system and of the 4-group. The logico-mathematical structures arise from the coordination of the actions of the subject and not from the pressures of physical objects.

3. The third fundamental factor is social interaction and transmission. Although necessary and essential, it also is insufficient by itself. Socialization is a structuration to which the individual contributes as much as he receives from it, whence the interdependence and isomorphism of "operation" and "cooperation." Even in the case of transmissions in which the subject appears most passive, such as school-teaching, social action is ineffective without an active assimilation by the child, which presupposes adequate operatory structures.

4. Three disparate factors do not add up to oriented development as simple and regular as that of the three great successive stages described. In view of the role of the subject and of the general coordinations of action in this development, one might be led to imagine a preestablished plan in the sense of apriority of internal finality. But an *a priori* plan could be realized biologically only through the mechanisms of innateness and maturation, and we have seen that they alone do not explain all the facts. Finality is a subjective notion, and an oriented development (a development that follows a direction: nothing more) does not necessarily presuppose a preestablished plan: for instance, the entropy in thermodynamics.

In the development of the child, there is no preestablished plan, but a gradual evolution in which each innovation is dependent upon the previous one. Adult thought might seem to provide a preestablished model, but the child does not understand adult thought until he has reconstructed it, and thought is itself the result of an evolution carried on by several generations, each of which has gone through childhood. Any explanation of the child's development must take into consideration two dimensions: an ontogenetic dimension and a social dimension (in the sense of the transmission of the successive work of generations). However, the problem is somewhat analogous in both cases, for in both the central question concerns the internal mechanism of all constructivism.

An internal mechanism (though it cannot be reduced to heredity alone and has no preestablished plan, since there is in fact construction) is observable at the time of each partial construction and each transition from one stage to the next. It is a process of equilibrium, not in the sense of a simple balance of forces, as in mechanics, or an increase of entropy, as in thermodynamics, but in the sense—which has now been brought out so clearly by cybernetics—of self-regulation; that is, a series of active compensations on the part of the subject in response to external disturbances and an adjustment that is both retroactive (loop systems or feedbacks) and anticipatory, constituting a permanent system of compensations.

It may appear that these four major factors explain only the intellectual and cognitive evolution of the child and that the development of affectivity and motivation must be considered separately. It may even seem that affective, dynamic factors provide the key to all mental development and that in the last analysis it is the need to grow, to assert oneself, to love, and to be admired that constitutes the motive force of intelligence, as well as of behavior in its totality and in its increasing complexity.

As we have seen repeatedly, affectivity constitutes the energetics of behavior patterns whose cognitive aspect refers to the structures alone. There is no behavior pattern, however intellectual, which does not involve affective factors as motives; but, reciprocally, there can be no affective states without the intervention of perceptions or comprehensions which constitute their cognitive structure. Behavior is therefore of a piece, even if the structures do not explain its energetics and if, vice versa, its energetics do not account for its structures. The two aspects, affective and cognitive, are at the same time inseparable and irreducible.

It is precisely this unity of behavior which makes the factors in development common to both the cognitive and the affective aspects; and their irreducibility in no way rules out a functional parallelism which is rather striking even in details (as we have seen in connection with "object relations," interpersonal connections, and moral sentiments). Indeed, the sentiments involve incontestable hereditary (or instinctive) roots subject to maturation. They become diversified in the course of actual experience. They derive a fundamental enrichment from interpersonal or social exchange. But, beyond these three factors, they unquestionably involve conflicts or crises and reequilibrations, for the formation of personality is dominated by the search for a coherence and an organization of values that will prevent internal conflicts (or seek them, but for the sake of new systematic perspectives such as "ambiguity" and other subjective syntheses). Even if we disregard the function of the moral sentiments, with their normative equilibrium (in which they are so near to the operatory structures), it is impossible to interpret the development of affective life and of motivations without stressing the all-important role of self-regulations, whose importance, moreover, all the schools have emphasized, albeit under various names.

This interpretation can claim to give a fairly good account of the known facts, first of all because an equilibration is necessary to reconcile the roles of maturation, experience with objects, and social experience. Then, too, the sensori-motor structures proceed from initial rhythms to regulations, and from regulations to the beginnings of reversibility. The regulations are directly dependent on the equilibration factor, and all later development (whether of thought, of moral reciprocity, or of cooperation) is a continuous process leading from the regulations to reversibility and to an extension of reversibility. Reversibility is a complete—that is, totally balanced—system of compensations in which each transformation is balanced by the possibility of an inverse or a reciprocal.

Thus, equilibration by self-regulation constitutes the formative process of the structures we have described. Child psychology enables us to follow their step-by-step evolution, not in the abstract, but in the lived and living dialectic of subjects who are faced, in each generation, with endlessly recurring problems and who sometimes arrive at solutions that are slightly better than those of previous generations.

BIBLIOGRAPHY

Paul Fraisse and Jean Piaget, eds. *Experimental Psychology: Its Scope and Method.* Vol. VII: *Intelligence.* New York: Basic Books, 1969; London: Routledge and Kegan Paul, 1969. Vol. VI: *Perception.* New York: Basic Books; London: Routledge and Kegan Paul, in preparation (*La Perception,* Paris: Presses Universitaire de France, 1963).

Bärbel Inhelder and Jean Piaget. *The Growth of Logical Thinking from Childhood to Adolescence.* New York: Basic Books, 1958; London: Routledge and Kegan Paul, 1958.

Bärbel Inhelder and Jean Piaget. *The Early Growth of Logic in the Child: Classification and Seriation.* London: Routledge and Kegan Paul, 1964.

Jean Piaget and Bärbel Inhelder. *Le Développement des quantités chez l'enfant.* Neuchâtel: Delachaux et Niestlé. 1941, 2nd ed. 1962; London: Routledge and Kegan Paul, in preparation.

Jean Piaget. *The Moral Judgment of the Child.* London: Routledge and Kegan Paul, 1932; Glencoe, Ill.: The Free Press, 1948.

Jean Piaget. *The Psychology of Intelligence.* New York: Harcourt, Brace, 1950; London: Routledge and Kegan Paul, 1950.

Jean Piaget. *The Child's Conception of the World.* London: Routledge and Kegan Paul, 1951.

Jean Piaget and Bärbel Inhelder. *La Genèse de l'idée de hasard chez l'enfant.* Paris: Presses Universitaire de France, 1951.

Jean Piaget. *Judgment and Reasoning in the Child.* London: Routledge and Kegan Paul, 1951.

Jean Piaget. *Play, Dreams and Imitation in Childhood.* New York: W. W. Norton, 1951; London: Routledge and Kegan Paul, 1951.

Jean Piaget and Alina Szeminska. *The Child's Conception of Number.* New York: Humanities Press, 1952; London: Routledge and Kegan Paul, 1952.

Jean Piaget. *The Language and Thought of the Child.* London: Routledge and Kegan Paul, 1952.

Jean Piaget. *The Origins of Intelligence in Children.* New York: International Universities Press, 1952; London: Routledge and Kegan Paul, 1953.

Jean Piaget. *The Construction of Reality in the Child.* New York: Basic Books, 1954; London: Routledge and Kegan Paul, 1955.

Jean Piaget and Bärbel Inhelder. *The Child's Conception of Space.* London: Routledge and Kegan Paul, 1956.

Jean Piaget. *Logic and Psychology.* London: Manchester University Press, 1953; New York: Basic Books, 1957.

Jean Piaget, Bärbel Inhelder, and Alina Szeminska. *The Child's Conception of Geometry.* New York: Basic Books, 1960; London: Routledge and Kegan Paul, 1960.

Jean Piaget and Bärbel Inhelder. *L'Image mentale chez l'enfant.* Paris: Presses Universitaires de France, 1966. New York: Basic Books; London: Routledge and Kegan Paul, in preparation.

Jean Piaget. *Six Psychological Studies.* New York: Random House, 1968.

Jean Piaget. *The Child's Conception of Movement and Speed.* New York: Basic Books, 1969; London: Routledge and Kegan Paul, 1969.

Jean Piaget. *The Mechanisms of Perception.* New York: Basic Books, 1969; London: Routledge and Kegan Paul, 1969.

OF RELATED INTEREST

Ruth M. Beard. *An Outline of Piaget's Developmental Psychology for Students and Teachers.* New York: Basic Books, 1969; London: Routledge and Kegan Paul, 1969.

INDEX

Aboudaram, M., 79
accommodation, 6
acquisition, 7, 8
action: decentering of, 94,
   98; and memory, 81 *n*; and
   mental representation, 93;
   and operations, 92, 96–97;
   and structuration, 4, 6, 44;
   transition to concrete operations, 93–96; reversibility,
   96, 97
adolescence: algebra of potentialities, 131; characteristics of, 130; crisis theories
   of, 151 *n*, and propositional
   operations, 135–136; and social awareness, 150–151;
adualism, 22–24
adultomorphism, 21
affectivity: in adolescence,
   149–151; and adualism, 22–
   24; and adultomorphism, 21;
   and causality, 24; and cognition, 21, 26–27; at concrete
   operations level, 149; decentering of, 25–26, 129; devel-

opment of, 114–117; and
   drawing, 68 *n*; and energetics, 21; in institutionalized
   children, 27; at formal operations level, 149–151; and
   mental development, 157–
   159; nature of, 21–22; and
   psychoanalysis, 149, 150;
   and reactions to persons, 24–
   25; and symbolic play, 60 *n*,
   115–116
Affolter, F., 88
alter-ego, 25
Anthony, E. J., 26 *n*
aphasia, 51
Aristotle, on induction, 148 *n*
Aserinsky, E., 69 *n*
assimilation: defined, 6; and
   insight, 12; and intelligence,
   5–6; and play, 61 *n*; recognitive, 7; and reflex, 8–9;
   schemes of, 6, 11, 12; and
   stimulus-response, 4–5; and
   theory of associationism, 5–
   6, 8; and thumbsucking, 7–8